HOLY ROSARY

THROUGH THE VISIONS OF BLESSED
ANNE CATHERINE EMMERICH

꘠

Blessed

ANNE CATHERINE EMMERICH

From the Translation by

VERY REV. K. E. SCHMOGER, C.SS.R

Compiled and Edited by

FR. MARK HIGGINS

CATHOLIC WAY
PUBLISHING

Published in 2019 by Catholic Way Publishing.
Cover & Book design by Catholic Way Publishing.

The text used is the translation from the original German by the Very Rev. K. E. Schmoger, C.SS. R. minor alterations have been made for the sake of clarity, particularly with regards to words that have long since become archaic since his 1870 translation. Let us pray for the soul of this priest, who accomplished such a marvellous and lengthy task, and whom has now been forgotten to history, a fate which will befall each one of us, in our due time.

This work is published for the greater glory of Jesus Christ through His most holy mother Mary and for the sanctification of the Church militant.

ISBN-13: 978-1-78379-510-9

10 9 8 7 6 5 4 3 2 1

Available in E-Book.

www.catholicwaypublishing.com
London, England, UK
2019

CONTENTS

THE HOLY ROSARY THROUGH THE VISIONS OF BLESSED ANNE CATHERINE EMMERICH

❧

INTRODUCTION

BLESSED ANNE CATHERINE EMMERICH (8TH SEPTEMBER 1774-9th February 1824), the great German mystic, spent her life hidden in devout contemplation. This poor woman was despised by the world and passed her days in monastic seclusion, initially in an Augustinian convent, and then later, after her convent was dissolved, in the house of a widow. Anne suffered in body and spirit from various supernatural ailments, culminating in the experience of the stigmata.

From her earliest years Anne was graced with an extraordinarily sensitive soul and an almost native intimacy with things of Almighty God, such that she befriended her guardian angel, and even experienced, while in prayer, sensory visions of the lives of Our Blessed Lord, His holy mother, and the many other characters of salvation history.

The records of her visions have been published and are available in both paper and e-book formats through The Catholic Way press. These revelations are a lens into the truths of Sacred Tradition, and they provide us with many details that have been unrecorded in Sacred Scripture. Many works of art, literature and popular devotional works have drawn important details from the revelations given to this humble German religious sister, whilst at the same time, some of the gems disclosed to Blessed Anne Catherine have remained concealed, little known of, and seldom talked about even among pious circles. Some readers may initially find some of the revelations disclosed within these rosary mysteries to be seemingly 'fantastic', that is, very beyond the ordinary, whenever such a thought arises, I beg you, allow yourself to ponder the mystery, and always remember we are not treating with events of a purely human content, no, indeed, were are dealing with events that are seeped in the supernatural. If the lives of the great saints, saints like St. Padre Pio, St. Teresa of Avila, St. Gemma Galgani and many others, are filled with mystical phenomena, would it not be natural to presume that the Holy of Holies, the God-man, and His holy mother, would have lives on a spiritual plane far above our own, and inhabiting an environment filled with the angelic, the opposition of the demonic, and the excitement of created nature recognising their owners and their lords.

The compiler of this short book makes no claims of originality, no claims of expertise, no claims of invention, he solely claims to have carefully reviewed the writings of this devout and pious woman and to have arranged them in such a manner as to facilitate the recitation of the Holy Rosary. For some of the mysteries our saint has offered us many beautiful details, and it is the editor's hope that meditating on these short segments will inspire you to enter more fully into her writings and indeed, perhaps to prepare a similar compilation, far greater it is to be hoped, than the one provided here.

If you are praying the rosary alone, it is suggested that you read the initial text before commencing the Our Father, afterwards the ten paragraphs of additional meditation could either be read before or during each Hail Mary. In a group setting a leader is required to read aloud each paragraph and commence each Hail Mary. The experience of the editor is that, in private use, with a prayerful silent reading of each passage, to say five mysteries will take at least 30 minutes and for some people closer to 45. If you feel the movements of grace pulling you into a simpler contemplation of a mystery as you read a paragraph, do not resist the Holy Spirit, and allow yourself to be at rest in the affect (the response of the heart) which Almighty God is stirring from within your soul.

Let us pray for Our Lady's intentions, for the conversion of the whole world to the one true Catholic Faith, for the sanctification of the clergy and for the relief of the suffering souls in purgatory.

In addition to the Fifteen Mysteries of the Holy Rosary, meditations are also included for those who wish to consider the mysteries proposed by Pope John Paul II, the Mysteries of Light, and, additionally a further set of mysteries prepared by the author, the Hopeful Mysteries. These further mysteries allow the reader to contemplate additional material offered to us by our visionary and cover events prior to the Joyful Mysteries, these are given as- The creation, the promise of the Redeemer and Co-Redemptrix to our first parents, the birth of the Immaculate Virgin Mary, the presentation of Mary in the temple, and the chaste espousals of Mary and Joseph.

It is customary to commence the Holy Rosary with the Sign of the Cross, the Apostles Creed, and then, for the intentions of the Holy Father, an Our Father, a Hail Mary, and a Glory be to the Father. After completing five mysteries we then say some concluding prayers centred around the Hail Holy Queen, these are contained at the end of this short work.

THE JOYFUL MYSTERIES

❧

The Annunciation

THE FRUIT OF THIS MYSTERY:

THE GIFT OF PIETY

HERE IN NAZARETH IT IS OTHERWISE THAN IN JERUSA-
lem, where the women must remain in the outer court and
may not enter the Temple, where only the priests may go into
the Holy Place. Here in Nazareth, here in this church, a

virgin is herself the Temple, and the Most Holy is within her, and the high priest is within her, and she alone is with Him. O, how lovely and wonderful that is, and yet so simple and natural! The words of David in the 45th Psalm were fulfilled: 'The Most High has sanctified His own tabernacle; God is in the midst thereof, it shall not be moved'.

OUR FATHER

Our Father who art in heaven, hallowed be thy name. Thy kingdom come. Thy will be done, on earth as it is in heaven. Give us this day our daily bread; and forgive us our trespasses, as we forgive those who trespass against us; and lead us not into temptation, but deliver us from evil.

HAIL MARY X10

Hail Mary full of Grace, the Lord is with thee. Blessed are thou among women and blessed is the fruit of thy womb Jesus. Holy Mary Mother of God, pray for us sinners now and at the hour of our death Amen.

MEDITATIONS

1) Soon after the Blessed Virgin's marriage I saw her in Joseph's house in Nazareth, where I was taken by my guide. Joseph had gone away with two donkeys—I think to fetch either his tools or something that he had inherited. He seemed to me to be on his way home. The Blessed Virgin

came in and went behind the screen before her bed, where she put on a long white woollen praying-robe with a broad girdle, and covered her head with a yellowish white veil.

2) Mary let the veil fall over her face and crossed her hands (but, not her fingers) before her breast. I saw her fervently praying thus for a long time, with her face raised to heaven. She was imploring God for redemption, for the promised King, and beseeching Him that her prayer might have some share in sending Him. She knelt long in an ecstasy of prayer; then she bowed her head onto her breast.

3) But now at her right hand there poured down such a mass of light in a slanting line from the ceiling of the room that I felt myself pressed back by it against the wall near the door.

4) I saw in this light a shining white youth, with flowing yellow hair, floating down before her. It was the Angel Gabriel. He gently moved his arms away from his body as he spoke to her. I saw the words issuing from his mouth like shining letters; I read them and I heard them.

5) Mary turned her veiled head slightly towards the right, but she was shy and did not look up. But the angel went on speaking, and as if at his command Mary turned her face a little towards him, raised her veil slightly, and answered. The angel again spoke, and Mary lifted her veil, looked at him, and answered with the holy words: "Behold the handmaid of the Lord, be it done to me according to your word".

6) The Blessed Virgin was wrapped in ecstasy. The room was filled with light; I no longer saw the glimmer of the burning lamp, I no longer saw the ceiling of the room. Heaven seemed to open, a path of light made me look up above the angel, and at the source of this stream of light I saw a figure of the Holy Trinity in the form of a triangular radiance streaming in upon itself. In this I recognised—what can only be adored and never expressed—Almighty God, Father, Son and Holy Ghost, and yet only one, God Almighty.

7) As soon as the Blessed Virgin had spoken the words, "Be it done to me according to your word", I saw the Holy Ghost in the appearance of a winged figure, but not in the form of a dove as usually represented. The head was like the face of a man, and light was spread like wings beside the figure, from whose breast and hands I saw three streams of light pouring down towards the right side of the Blessed Virgin and meeting as they reached her. This light streaming in upon her right side caused the Blessed Virgin to become completely transfused with radiance and as though transparent; all that was opaque seemed to vanish like darkness before this light. In this moment she was so penetrated with light that nothing dark or concealing remained in her; her whole form was shining and transfused with light.

8) While I was seeing all this in Mary's chamber, I had a strange personal sensation. I was in a state of constant fear, as if I was being pursued, and I suddenly saw a hideous serpent crawling through the house and up the steps to the door by

which I was standing. The horrible creature had made its way as far as the third step when the light poured down on the Blessed Virgin. The serpent was three or four feet long, had a broad flat head and under its breast were two short skinny paws, clawed like bat's wings, on which it pushed itself forward. It was spotted with all kinds of hideous colours, and reminded me of the serpent in the Garden of Eden, only fearfully deformed. When the angel disappeared from the Blessed Virgin's room, he trod on this monster's head as it lay before the door, and it screamed in so ghastly a way that I shuddered. Then I saw three spirits appear who drove the monster out in front of the house with blows and kicks.

9) After the angel had disappeared, I saw the Blessed Virgin wrapped in the deepest ecstasy. I saw that she recognised the Incarnation of the promised Redeemer within herself in the form of a tiny human figure of light, perfectly formed in all its parts down to its tiny fingers.

10) It was at midnight that I saw this mystery happen. After a little while Anna with the other women came into Mary's room. They had been wakened by a strange commotion in nature. A cloud of light had appeared above the house. When they saw the Blessed Virgin kneeling under the lamp in an ecstasy of prayer, they respectfully withdrew.

GLORY BE TO THE FATHER

Glory be to the Father and to the Son and to the Holy Spirit. As it was in the beginning is now, and ever shall be, world without end. Amen.

THE FATIMA PRAYER

O my Jesus, forgive us our sins, save us from the fires of hell, and lead all souls to Heaven, especially those in most need of Your Mercy.

The Visitation

THE FRUIT OF THIS MYSTERY:
DEVOTION TO OUR LORD JESUS CHRIST, TRULY
PRESENT IN THE MOST HOLY SACRAMENT OF
THE ALTAR.

WITH THE ANGEL'S SALUTATION THE BLESSED VIRGIN was
consecrated as the Church. With the words "Behold the

handmaid of the Lord, be it done to me according to your word", the Word entered into her, saluted by the Church, by His maidservant. God was now in His Temple, Mary was now the Temple and the Ark of the New Covenant. Elizabeth's greeting and the movement of John beneath his mother's heart was the first act of worship of the community in the presence of this Holy Thing. When the Blessed Virgin uttered the Magnificat, the Church of the New Covenant, of the new Espousals, celebrated for the first time the fulfilment of the divine promises of the Old Covenant, of the old Espousals, and poured forth thanks with a Te Deum laudamus. Ah, who can express the wonder of seeing the devotion of the Church towards the Saviour even before His Birth!

OUR FATHER

Our Father who art in heaven, hallowed be thy name. Thy kingdom come. Thy will be done, on earth as it is in heaven. Give us this day our daily bread; and forgive us our trespasses, as we forgive those who trespass against us; and lead us not into temptation, but deliver us from evil.

HAIL MARY XIO

Hail Mary full of Grace, the Lord is with thee. Blessed are thou among women and blessed is the fruit of thy womb Jesus. Holy Mary Mother of God, pray for us sinners now and at the hour of our death Amen.

MEDITATIONS

1) Some days after the Annunciation, St. Joseph returned to Nazareth and made further arrangements for working at his craft in the house. He had never lived in Nazareth before and had not spent more than a few days there. Joseph knew nothing of the Incarnation; Mary was the Mother of the Lord, but also the handmaid of the Lord, and she kept His secret in all humility.

2) When the Blessed Virgin felt that the Word was made Flesh in her, she was conscious of a great desire to pay an immediate visit to her cousin Elizabeth at Juttah near Hebron, whom the angel had told her was now six months with child.

3) Zechariah's house was on the top of a hill by itself. Other houses stood in groups round about. Not far off a biggish stream flowed down from the mountain. It seemed to me to be the moment when Zechariah was returning home from the Passover at Jerusalem. I saw Elizabeth, moved by great longing, going out of her house for a considerable distance on the way to Jerusalem; and I saw how alarmed Zechariah was, as he made his way home, to meet Elizabeth on the road so far from home in her condition. She told him that she was so agitated in her heart because she could not help thinking all the time that her cousin Mary of Nazareth was coming to her.

4) Zechariah tried to remove this impression from her mind and explained to her, by signs and by writing on a tablet, how unlikely it was that a newly married woman should undertake so long a journey just then. They went back to the house together. Elizabeth was, however, unable to abandon her expectation, for she had learnt in a dream that one of her family had become the mother of the promised Messiah. She had at once thought of Mary, had longed to see her, and had in spirit perceived her in the distance on her way to her.

5) On the following day she sat there for a long time waiting and gazing out of the house, watching for the coming visitor. Then she got up and went a long way on the road to meet her. Her head was wrapped in a veil. She only knew the Blessed Virgin by hearsay. Mary saw her from far off and recognised her at once. She ran to meet her, while Joseph discreetly remained behind.

6) They greeted each other warmly with outstretched hands, and at that moment I saw a shining brightness in the Blessed Virgin and as it were a ray of light passing from her to Elizabeth, filling the latter with wonderful joy. They did not stay near the people in the houses, but went, holding each other by the arm, through the outer court towards the house. At the door Elizabeth once more made Mary welcome, and they then went in.

7) Again I saw a radiance stream from Mary into Elizabeth, whereby the latter was transfused with light. Her heart was

filled with holy joy. She stepped back, her hand raised, and exclaimed full of humility, joy, and exaltation: "Blessed are you among women and blessed is the fruit of your womb. And whence is this to me that the mother of my Lord should come to me? For behold as the voice of your salutation sounded in my ears, the infant in my womb leaped for joy. And blessed are you that have believed, because those things shall be accomplished that were spoken to you by the Lord".

8) As she said the last words she led Mary into the little room which she had prepared, so that she might sit down and rest after her journey. It was only a few paces away. Mary let go Elizabeth's arm, which she had clasped, crossed her hands over her breast and uttered the Magnificat with exaltation. I saw that Elizabeth followed in prayer the whole of the Magnificat in a similar state of exaltation. O, I was so blissfully happy, I prayed with them the whole time, and then I sat down near at hand: oh, I was so happy!

9) Tonight, as I watched the two holy women at their prayers, I had many visions and explanations of the Magnificat and of the coming of the Blessed Sacrament in the present condition of the Blessed Virgin. From the passage in the Magnificat "He has shown might in His arm" onwards there appeared to me all kinds of pictures from the Old Testament symbolic of the most holy Sacrament of the Altar. I saw many things from Abraham to Isaiah and from Isaiah to the Blessed Virgin, and in everything I always saw the coming of the

Blessed Sacrament to the Church of Jesus Christ, who was Himself still resting under His Mother's heart.

10) During Mary's prayer I saw a continuous succession of all her ancestors. In the course of time there followed each other three times fourteen marriages, in each of which the son succeeded directly to the father: and from each of these marriages I saw a ray of light projected towards Mary as she stood there in prayer. The whole vision grew before my eyes like a family tree made by branches of light becoming ever nobler and nobler, until at last, in a more clearly defined place in this tree of light, I saw shine forth more brightly the holy and immaculate flesh and blood of Mary, from which God was to become Man. I prayed to her in yearning and hope, as full of joy as a child who sees the Christmas tree towering above him. It was all a picture of the coming of Jesus Christ in the Flesh and of His most holy Sacrament.

GLORY BE TO THE FATHER

Glory be to the Father and to the Son and to the Holy Spirit. As it was in the beginning is now, and ever shall be, world without end. Amen.

THE FATIMA PRAYER

O my Jesus, forgive us our sins, save us from the fires of hell, and lead all souls to Heaven, especially those in most need of Your Mercy.

The Nativity of Jesus Christ

THE FRUIT OF THIS MYSTERY:
PERFECT CONFORMITY WITH THE HOLY WILL OF GOD.

IN THESE PICTURES OF CHRIST'S BIRTH, WHICH I SEE AS
an historical event and not just as a Feast of the Church, I do
not see such radiant and ecstatic joy in nature as I do on
Christmas night when the vision that I see expresses an

interior significance. I saw in this vision an unwonted joy and an extraordinary movement at midnight in many places even to the uttermost parts of the earth. I saw the hearts of many good men filled with joyful yearning, while all the wicked were overcome by great fear. I saw many animals filled with joy; in some places I saw flowers, herbs, and shrubs shooting up, and trees drinking in refreshment and scattering sweet scents. I saw many springs of water gush forth and increase.

OUR FATHER

Our Father who art in heaven, hallowed be thy name. Thy kingdom come. Thy will be done, on earth as it is in heaven. Give us this day our daily bread; and forgive us our trespasses, as we forgive those who trespass against us; and lead us not into temptation, but deliver us from evil.

HAIL MARY XIO

Hail Mary full of Grace, the Lord is with thee. Blessed are thou among women and blessed is the fruit of thy womb Jesus. Holy Mary Mother of God, pray for us sinners now and at the hour of our death Amen.

MEDITATIONS

1) I saw the Blessed Virgin in the house. She was far advanced in pregnancy, and sat in a room working with several other women. Anna thought that Mary would be in her

house for the birth of her child, and that all her relations would come to visit her there, she made all the preparations in a very lavish manner, with specially beautiful coverlets and rugs.

2) Today I saw the Blessed Virgin and her mother Anna in the house in Nazareth, where Joseph revealed to them what had been told him the previous night. Thereupon they returned to Anna's house, and I saw them preparing to leave immediately. Anna was distressed. The Blessed Virgin must have known that she was to bear her child in Bethlehem, but had been silent out of humility. She knew it from the writings of the Prophets about the birth of the Messiah, all of which she treasured in her little cupboard at Nazareth.

3) This morning I saw the holy travellers arrive at an open field called Ginim, six hours journey from Nazareth, where the angel had appeared to Joseph two days before. Anna had a pasture here and the menservants were told to fetch the young she-ass which Joseph was to take with him. She sometimes ran in front of them and sometimes beside them. Anna and Mary Cleophas here took a tender farewell of the travellers and returned home with the menservants.

4) I saw the Holy Family some hours journey beyond this last place, going at night towards a mountain through a very cold valley. It looked as if there was hoar-frost on the ground. Joseph spoke to Mary about the good lodging which he hoped to find for her in Bethlehem. He said he knew of a

house with very good people where they would find a comfortable lodging at very little cost. It was, he said, better to pay something than to be taken in for nothing. He spoke highly of Bethlehem in general, and comforted the Blessed Virgin in every possible way. (This upset me, because I knew well that things would turn out quite differently. Even this holy man, you see, indulged in human hopes).

5) Joseph came back to her in great distress; he had found no shelter. His friends, of whom he had spoken to the Blessed Virgin, would hardly recognise him. He was in tears and Mary comforted him. He said he had had no success, but he knew of one place outside the town, belonging to the shepherds, who often went there when coming with their flocks to the town. There they would, in any case, find a shelter. He said that he knew the place from childhood; when his brothers had tormented him, he had often escaped there to hide from them and to say his prayers. I was told much that had happened in the Cave of the Nativity of symbolical and prophetical significance in Old Testament times.

6) Mary had told St. Joseph that tonight at midnight would be the hour of the child's birth, for then the nine months since the Annunciation would have been completed. She begged him to do all that was possible on his part so that they might show as much honour as they could to the child promised by God and supernaturally conceived. She asked him, too, to join with her in praying for the hard-hearted people who had refused to give them shelter.

7) Joseph stood at the entrance of the cave where he had prepared his sleeping place. Looking towards the Blessed Virgin, he saw her with her face turned towards the east, kneeling on the bed facing away from him. He saw her as it were surrounded by flames, the whole cave was as if filled with supernatural light. He gazed at her like Moses when he saw the burning bush; then he went into his little cell in holy awe and threw himself on his face in prayer.

8) I saw the radiance round the Blessed Virgin ever growing greater. The light of the lamps which Joseph had lit was no longer visible. The Blessed Virgin knelt on her rug in an ample ungirt robe spread out round her, her face turned towards the east. At midnight she was rapt in an ecstasy of prayer. I saw her lifted from the earth, so that I saw the ground beneath her. Her hands were crossed on her breast. The radiance about her increased; everything, even things without life, were in a joyful inner motion, the stones of the roof, of the walls, and of the floor of the cave became as it were alive in the light. Then I no longer saw the roof of the cave; a pathway of light opened above Mary, rising with ever-increasing glory towards the height of heaven. In this pathway of light there was a wonderful movement of glories interpenetrating each other, and, as they approached, appearing more clearly in the form of choirs of heavenly spirits.

9) The Blessed Virgin, borne up in ecstasy, was now gazing downwards, adoring her God, whose Mother she had become and who lay on the earth before her in the form of a helpless

newborn child. I saw our Redeemer as a tiny child, shining with a light that overpowered all the surrounding radiance, and lying on the carpet at the Blessed Virgin's knees. The Blessed Virgin remained for some time rapt in ecstasy. I saw her laying a cloth over the Child, but at first she did not touch Him or take Him up. After some time I saw the Child Jesus move and heard Him cry. Then Mary seemed to come to herself, and she took the Child up from the carpet, wrapping Him in the cloth which covered Him and held Him in her arms to her breast. She sat there enveloping herself and the Child completely in her veil, and I think Mary suckled the Redeemer. I saw angels round her in human forms, lying on their faces and adoring the Child.

10) It might have been an hour after His birth when Mary called St. Joseph, who was still lying in prayer. When he came near, he threw himself down on his face in devout joy and humility. It was only when Mary begged him to take to his heart, in joy and thankfulness, the holy present of the Most High God, that he stood up, took the Child Jesus in his arms, and praised God with tears of joy. Then I saw Mary and Joseph sitting side by side on the bare earth with their feet under them. They did not speak, and seemed both to be sunk in meditation. On the carpet before Mary lay the newborn Jesus in swaddling-clothes, a little Child, beautiful and radiant as lightning. Ah, I thought, this place enshrines the salvation of the whole world, and no one guesses it.

GLORY BE TO THE FATHER

Glory be to the Father and to the Son and to the Holy Spirit. As it was in the beginning is now, and ever shall be, world without end. Amen.

THE FATIMA PRAYER

O my Jesus, forgive us our sins, save us from the fires of hell, and lead all souls to Heaven, especially those in most need of Your Mercy.

The Purification of Mary and the Presentation of the Infant Christ in the Temple

THE FRUIT OF THIS MYSTERY:
HOLY PREPARATION TO MEET THE LORD.

THE DAYS BEING NEARLY FULFILLED WHEN THE BLESSED
Virgin must, according to the Law, present and redeem her

firstborn in the Temple, all was prepared for the Holy Family's journey first to the Temple and then to their home in Nazareth. Mary was praying all the time, and seemed to be preparing herself for the coming ceremony. It was revealed to me at the same time how one should prepare oneself for receiving Holy Communion.

OUR FATHER

Our Father who art in heaven, hallowed be thy name. Thy kingdom come. Thy will be done, on earth as it is in heaven. Give us this day our daily bread; and forgive us our trespasses, as we forgive those who trespass against us; and lead us not into temptation, but deliver us from evil.

HAIL MARY XIO

Hail Mary full of Grace, the Lord is with thee. Blessed are thou among women and blessed is the fruit of thy womb Jesus. Holy Mary Mother of God, pray for us sinners now and at the hour of our death Amen.

MEDITATIONS

1) I had a vision of the aged Simeon. He was a thin, very old man with a short beard. He was an ordinary priest, was married, and had three grown-up sons. I saw Simeon, who lived close to the Temple, going through a narrow dark passage in the Temple walls into a small vaulted cell, built in

the thickness of the wall. The aged Simeon knelt in this little cell, rapt in prayer. Then the appearance of an angel stood before him. and warned him to take heed of the little child who should be first presented early next morning, for this was the Messiah for whom he had so long yearned. After he had seen Him, he would soon die. I saw this so plainly; the room was illuminated, and the holy old man was radiant with joy. Then I saw him going to his house and telling his wife with great joy what had been announced to him. After his wife had gone to bed, I saw Simeon betake himself to prayer again.

2) This morning, while it was still dark, I saw the Holy Family, accompanied by the people of the inn, leaving the inn and going to Jerusalem to the Temple with the baskets of offerings and with the donkey laden for the journey. They went into a walled courtyard in the Temple. While Joseph and the innkeeper stabled the donkey in a shed, the Blessed Virgin and her Child were kindly received by an aged woman and led into the Temple by a covered passage. A light was carried, for it was still dark. No sooner had they entered this passage than the aged priest Simeon came, full of expectation, towards the Blessed Virgin.

3) The Blessed Virgin was led by her guide to the outer courts of the Temple where the ceremony took place, and she was here received by Noemi, her former teacher, and Anna, who both lived on this side of the Temple. Anna, to whom Joseph gave the basket with the offerings, followed her with

Noemi. The doves were in the lower part of the basket; above them was a compartment with fruit. Joseph went by another door into the place set apart for men. Many lamps were burning on its walls, forming pyramids of light.

4) Simeon now approached the Blessed Virgin, in whose arms the Infant Jesus lay wrapped in a sky-blue covering, and led her through the railing to the table, where she laid the Child in the cradle. From this moment I saw an indescribable light filling the Temple. I saw that God Himself was in it, and above the Child I saw the heavens opening to disclose the Throne of the Holy Trinity.

5) Simeon remained standing with Mary before the table of offering, and the priest who stood behind it lifted the Infant Jesus from the cradle and held Him up towards the different sides of the Temple, making a long prayer the while. He then gave the Child to Simeon, who laid Him once more in Mary's arms and prayed over her and the Child from a scroll hanging on a stand beside him.

6) At the close of this ceremony, Simeon came up to where Mary was standing, took the Infant Jesus from her into his arms, speaking long and loudly over Him in raptures of joy and thanking God that He had fulfilled His Promise. He ended with his Nunc Dimittis. After the Presentation Joseph came up, and he and Mary listened with great reverence to Simeon's inspired words to the Blessed Virgin

7) When Simeon had finished speaking, the prophetess Anna was also filled with inspiration, and spoke long and loudly about the Infant Jesus, hailing His Mother as blessed. I saw that those who were present were greatly moved by all this, and the priests, too, seemed to hear something of what was happening; the hearts of all the bystanders were much moved, and all showed great reverence to the Child and His Mother. Mary was like a heavenly rose in radiance.

8) The Holy Family had, in appearance, made the most humble offering; but Joseph gave Anna and the aged Simeon many of the triangular pieces of gold in secret, to be used specially for poor girls who were being brought up in the Temple and could not afford the expense.

9) I saw that Simeon fell ill yesterday immediately on returning home after his prophecy at the Presentation of Jesus, but he spoke very joyfully with his wife and sons. Tonight I saw that today was to be the day of his death. Of the many things I saw I can only remember this much. Simeon, from the couch where he lay, spoke earnestly to his wife and children, telling them of the salvation that was come to Israel and of everything that the angel had announced to him. His joy was touching to behold.

10) I saw an altar appear in the centre of a Church—not an altar like those in our churches today, but just an altar. On this altar stood a little tree of the same kind as the Tree of Knowledge in the Garden of Eden, with broad hanging

leaves. Then I saw the Blessed Virgin rise before the altar with the Infant Jesus in her arms as if she had come up out of the earth; and I saw the tree on the altar bow before her and then wither away. I think that the withering of the Tree of Knowledge at Mary's appearance, and the passing of the Child on the altar into the Holy Trinity signified the reunion of mankind with God.

GLORY BE TO THE FATHER

Glory be to the Father and to the Son and to the Holy Spirit. As it was in the beginning is now, and ever shall be, world without end. Amen.

THE FATIMA PRAYER

O my Jesus, forgive us our sins, save us from the fires of hell, and lead all souls to Heaven, especially those in most need of Your Mercy.

The Finding of the
Boy Jesus in the Temple

THE FRUIT OF THIS MYSTERY:
SUBMISSION OF INTELLECT AND WILL TO THE
TEACHINGS OF JESUS CHRIST.

JESUS HAD BEEN TEACHING TWO HOURS, WHEN JOSEPH
and Mary entered the Temple. They inquired after their

Child of the Levites whom they knew, and received for answer that He was with the doctors in the lecture hall. But as they were not at liberty to enter that hall, they sent one of the Levites in to call Jesus. Jesus sent them word that He must first finish what He was doing. Mary was very much troubled at His not obeying at once, for this was the first time He had given His parents to understand that He had other commands than theirs to fulfil. Joseph was quite awed and astonished, but he kept a humble silence.

OUR FATHER

Our Father who art in heaven, hallowed be thy name. Thy kingdom come. Thy will be done, on earth as it is in heaven. Give us this day our daily bread; and forgive us our trespasses, as we forgive those who trespass against us; and lead us not into temptation, but deliver us from evil.

HAIL MARY XIO

Hail Mary full of Grace, the Lord is with thee. Blessed are thou among women and blessed is the fruit of thy womb Jesus. Holy Mary Mother of God, pray for us sinners now and at the hour of our death Amen.

MEDITATIONS

1) I saw Jesus assisting His parents in every possible way, and also on the street and wherever opportunity offered, cheerful-

ly, eagerly, and obligingly helping everyone. He assisted His foster-father in his trade, or devoted Himself to prayer and contemplation. He was a model for all the children of Nazareth. From His twelfth year, Jesus was always like a teacher among His companions. He often sat among them instructing them or walked about the country with them.

2) Jesus was tall and slender with a delicate face and a beaming countenance and though pale, He was healthy-looking. His perfectly straight, golden hair was parted over His high, open forehead and fell upon His shoulders. He wore a long, light-brownish grey tunic, which reached to His feet, the sleeves rather wide around the hand. At the age of eight years, Jesus went for the first time with His parents to Jerusalem for the Pasch, and every succeeding year He did the same.

3) In those first visits, Jesus had already excited attention in Jerusalem among the friends with whom He and His parents stayed, also among the priests and doctors. They spoke of the pious, intelligent Child, of Joseph's extraordinary Son, just as amongst us one might, at the annual pilgrimages, notice in particular this or that modest, holy-looking person, this or that clever peasant child, and recognise him again the next year. So Jesus had already some acquaintances in the city when, in His twelfth year, with their friends and their sons, He accompanied His parents to Jerusalem. His parents were accustomed to walk with the people from their own part of the country, and they knew that Jesus, who now made the

journey for the fifth time, always went with the other youths from Nazareth.

4) But this time Jesus had, on the return journey not far from the Mount of Olives, separated from His companions, who all thought that He had joined His parents who were following. Jesus had, however, gone to that side of Jerusalem nearest to Bethlehem, to the inn at which the Holy Family before Mary's Purification had put up. Mary and Joseph thought Him on ahead with the other Nazarenes, while these latter thought that He was following with His parents.

5) When at last the two parties reunited, the anxiety of Mary and Joseph at His absence was very great. They returned at once to Jerusalem, making inquiries after Him on the way and everywhere in the city itself. But they could not find Him, since He had not been where they usually stayed. Jesus had slept at the inn before the Bethlehem gate, where the people knew Him and His parents.

6) The boy Jesus had joined with other young men in Jerusalem, he had gone with them to two schools of the city, the first day to one, the second to another. On the morning of the third day, He had gone to a third school at the Temple, and in the afternoon into the Temple itself where His parents found Him. These schools were all different, and not all exactly schools of the Law. Other branches were taught in them. The last mentioned was in the neighbourhood of the Temple and from it the Levites and priests were chosen.

7) Jesus by His questions and answers so astonished and embarrassed the doctors and rabbis of all these schools that they resolved, on the afternoon of the third day, in the public lecture hall of the Temple and in presence of the rabbis most deeply versed in the various sciences "to humble the Boy Jesus". The scribes and doctors had concerted the plan together; for, although pleased at first, they had in the end become vexed at Him

8) They met in the public lecture hall in the middle of the Temple porch in front of the Sanctuary, in the round place where later Jesus also taught. There I saw Jesus sitting in a large chair which He did not, by a great deal, fill. Around Him was a crowd of aged Jews in priestly robes. They were listening attentively, and appeared to be perfectly furious. I feared they would lay hands upon Him. He discoursed with the same facility upon astronomy, architecture, agriculture, geometry, arithmetic, jurisprudence and, in fine, upon every subject proposed to Him. He applied all so skilfully to the Law and the Promise, to the Prophecies, to the Temple, to the mysteries of worship and sacrifice that His hearers, surprised and confounded, passed successively from astonishment and admiration to fury and shame. They were enraged at hearing some things that they never before knew, and at hearing others that they had never before understood.

9) The boy Jesus continued to teach for another hour, and then He left the hall, here He met His parents in the porch of Israel, the women's porch. His hearers were left confounded,

confused, and enraged. Mary, however, drawing near to Jesus, said, "Child, why have you done this to us? Behold, Thy father and I have sought You sorrowing!"

10) But Jesus answered gravely, "Why have you sought Me? Do you not know that I must be about My Father's business?" But they did not understand. They at once began with Him their journey home. The bystanders gazed at them in astonishment, and I was in dread lest they should lay hands upon the Boy, for I saw that some of them were full of rage. I wondered at their allowing the Holy Family to depart so peaceably. Although the crowd was dense, yet a wide path was made to permit the Holy Family to pass. I saw all the details and heard almost the whole of Jesus' teaching, but I cannot remember all. It made a great impression upon the scribes. Some recorded the affair as a notable event, while here and there it was whispered around, giving rise to all kinds of remarks and false reports. But the true statement, the scribes kept to themselves.

GLORY BE TO THE FATHER

Glory be to the Father and to the Son and to the Holy Spirit. As it was in the beginning is now, and ever shall be, world without end. Amen.

THE FATIMA PRAYER

O my Jesus, forgive us our sins, save us from the fires of hell, and lead all souls to Heaven, especially those in most need of Your Mercy.

CONCLUDING PRAYERS

Upon concluding the recitation of the Holy Rosary, the following prayers are customary, but others too may be added according to one's devotion and preference.

HAIL, HOLY QUEEN

Hail Holy Queen, Mother of Mercy, Hail our life our sweetness and our hope. To thee do we cry, poor banished children of Eve, to thee do we send up our sighs, mourning and weeping in this vale of tears. Turn then most gracious Advocate thine eyes of mercy towards us and after this our exile, show unto us the blessed fruit of thy womb, Jesus. O clement, O loving, O sweet Virgin Mary. Pray for us O holy Mother of God, that we may be made worthy of the promises of Christ.

Let us pray

O God Whose only begotten son by His life death and resurrection has purchased for us the rewards of eternal life, grant we beseech Thee that meditating on these mysteries of the most Holy Rosary of the Blessed Virgin Mary we may both imitate what they contain and obtain what they promise, through the same Christ our Lord. Amen.

PRAYER TO SAINT MICHAEL THE ARCHANGEL

Holy Michael, the Archangel, defend us in the day of battle. Be our safeguard against the wickedness and snares of the devil. May God rebuke him, we humbly pray; and do thou, O Prince of the heavenly hosts, by the power of God thrust down into hell Satan and all the evil spirits who wander through the world seeking the ruin of souls. Amen.

MEMORARE

Remember, O most gracious Virgin Mary, that never was it known that anyone who fled to thy protection, implored thy help, or sought thine intercession was left unaided. Inspired by this confidence, I fly unto thee, O Virgin of virgins, my mother; to thee do I come, before thee I stand, sinful and sorrowful. O Mother of the Word Incarnate, despise not my petitions, but in thy mercy hear and answer me. Amen.

May the Divine Assistance remain always with us, and may the souls of the faithful departed, through the mercy of God rest in peace. Amen.

THE SORROWFUL MYSTERIES

❧

The Agony in the Garden

THE FRUIT OF THIS MYSTERY:
HORROR OF SIN.

GETHSEMANE ON MOUNT OLIVET, WHERE THEY WERE going, was half an hour from the Upper Room. Jesus had sometimes passed the night with His Apostles there, instructing them. The garden contained some magnificent shrubbery and a great many fruit trees. The Garden of Olives was separated by a road from that of Gethsemane and was higher up the mountain. It was open, being surrounded by only a rampart of earth. It was smaller than the pleasure garden of Gethsemane, a retired corner of the mountain full of grottos, terraces, and olive trees. One side of it was kept in better order. The spot chosen by Jesus was the wildest. At first Jesus knelt calmly in prayer, but after awhile His soul shrank in affright from the multitude and heinousness of man's sins and ingratitude against God. So overpowering was the sadness, the agony of heart which fell upon Him that, trembling and shuddering, He prayed imploringly: "Abba, Father, if it be possible, remove this chalice from Me! My Father, all things are possible to You. Take this chalice from Me!" Then recovering Himself, He added: "But not what I will, but Your will be done". His will and the Father's were one. But now that through love He had delivered Himself up to the weakness of His human nature, He shuddered at the thought of death. Wringing His hands, He swayed from side to side, and the sweat of agony covered Him.

OUR FATHER

Our Father who art in heaven, hallowed be thy name. Thy kingdom come. Thy will be done, on earth as it is in heaven. Give us this day our daily bread; and forgive us our trespasses, as we forgive those who trespass against us; and lead us not into temptation, but deliver us from evil.

HAIL MARY XIO

Hail Mary full of Grace, the Lord is with thee. Blessed are thou among women and blessed is the fruit of thy womb

Jesus. Holy Mary Mother of God, pray for us sinners now and at the hour of our death Amen.

MEDITATIONS

1) Leaving the Upper Room, Jesus met His Mother, Mary Cleophas, and Magdalen, who besought Him imploringly not to go to the Mount of Olives, for it was reported that He would there be arrested. Jesus comforted them in a few words, and stepped quickly past them. It was then about nine o'clock. They went in haste down the road by which Peter and John had come up that morning to the Coenaculum, and directed their steps to Mount Olivet. He led The Eleven to the Mount of Olives by an unfrequented path through the Valley of Josaphat. As they left the house, I saw the moon, which was not yet quite full, rising above the mountain. While walking in the Valley of Josaphat with the Apostles, the Lord said that He would one day return hither, though not poor and powerless as He then was, to judge the world. Then would men tremble with fear and cry out: "O mountains, cover us!" But the disciples understood Him not. They thought, as several times before during the evening, that from weakness and exhaustion He was wandering in speech.

2) The Apostles were still full of the enthusiasm and devotion inspired by the reception of the Most Holy Sacrament, and the loving, solemn discourse of Jesus afterwards. They crowded eagerly around Him and expressed their love in different ways, protesting that they never could, they never would,

abandon Him. But as Jesus continued to speak in the same strain, Peter exclaimed: "Although all should be scandalised in You, I will never be scandalised in You!" The Lord replied: "Amen, I say to you that in this night before the cock crow, you will deny Me three time". They walked and paused alternately, and Jesus' sadness continued to increase. The Apostles tried to dissipate it by human arguments, assuring Him that just the opposite of what He dreaded would take place. But finding their efforts vain and fruitless, they grew weary, and began already to doubt and fall into temptation.

3) It was about nine o'clock when Jesus reached Gethsemane with the disciples. Darkness had fallen upon the earth, but the moon was lighting up the sky. Jesus was very sad. He announced to the Apostles the approach of danger, and they became uneasy. Jesus bade eight of them to remain in the Garden of Gethsemane, where there was a kind of summerhouse built of branches and foliage. "Remain here", He said, "while I go to My own place to pray". He took Peter, John, and James the Greater with Him, crossed the road, and went on for a few minutes, until He reached the Garden of Olives farther up the mountain. He was inexpressibly sad, for He felt His approaching agony and temptation. John asked how He, who had always consoled them, could now be so dejected. He replied: "My soul is sorrowful even unto death". He glanced around and on all sides saw anguish and temptation gathering about Him like dense clouds filled with frightful pictures. It was at that moment He said to the three Apostles:

"Remain here and watch with Me. Pray lest you enter into temptation!".

4) When Jesus left the Apostles, I saw a great number of frightful figures surrounding Him in an ever narrowing circle. His sorrow and anguish increased. He withdrew tremblingly into the back of the cave, like one seeking shelter from a violent tempest, and there He prayed. I saw the awful visions following Him into the grotto, and becoming ever more and more distinct. Ah! It was as if that narrow cave encompassed the horrible, the agonising vision of all the sins, with their delights and their punishments, committed from the Fall of our first parents till the end of the world; for it was here on Mount Olivet that Adam and Eve, driven from Paradise, had first descended upon the inhospitable earth, and in that very grotto had they in fear and alarm bewailed their misery.

5) To make satisfaction for the origin and development of all kinds of sin and guilty pleasures, the most merciful Jesus, through love for us sinners, received into His own Heart the root of all expiatory reconciliation and saving pains. He allowed those infinite sufferings in satisfaction for endless sins, like a thousand branched tree of pain, to pierce through, to extend through all the members of His Sacred Body, all the faculties of His holy Soul. Thus entirely given up to His Humanity, He fell on His face, calling upon God in unspeakable sorrow and anguish. He saw in countless forms all the sins of the world with their innate hideousness. He took all

upon Himself and offered Himself in His prayer to satisfy the justice of His Heavenly Father for all that guilt by His own sufferings.

6) Satan who, under a frightful form and with furious mockery, moved around among all this abomination, became at each moment more violently enraged against Him. He evoked before the eyes of His soul visions of the sins of men, one more frightful than the other, and constantly addressed to the Sacred Humanity of Jesus such words as, "What! Will you take all this also upon yourself? Are you ready to endure its penalty? How can you satisfy for this?"

7) Satan acted like the most crafty and subtle Pharisee. He reproached Jesus with causing Herod's massacre of the Holy Innocents, with exposing His parents to want and danger in Egypt, with not having rescued John the Baptist from death, with bringing about disunion in many families, with having protected degraded people, refusing to cure certain sick persons, with injuring the Gergeseans by permitting the possessed to overturn their vats and their swine to rush into the sea. He accused Him of the guilt of Mary Magdalen, since He had not prevented her relapse into sin; of neglecting His own family; of squandering the goods of others; and, in one word, all that the tempter would at the hour of death have brought to bear upon an ordinary mortal who, without a high and holy intention, had been mixed up in such affairs, Satan now suggested to the trembling soul of Jesus with the view of causing Him to waver. It was hidden from him that

Jesus was the Son of God, and he tempted Him as merely the most righteous of men.

8) While the adorable Humanity of Christ was thus agonising and writhing under this excess of suffering, I saw among the angels a feeling of compassion for Him. There seemed to be a pause, in which they appeared desirous of giving Him consolation, and I saw them praying to that effect before the throne of God. From that point in the heavens in which the sun appears between ten and eleven in the morning, a narrow path of light streamed toward Jesus, and on it I saw a file of angels coming down to Him. They imparted to Him fresh strength and vigour. The rest of the grotto was filled with the frightful and horrible visions of sin, and with the evil spirits mocking and tempting. Jesus took all upon Himself. In the midst of this confusion of abomination, His Heart, the only one that loved God and man perfectly, shrank in terror and anguish from the horror, the burden of all those sins. Ah, I saw there so many things! A whole year would not suffice to relate them!

9) Jesus arose, but His trembling knees could scarcely support Him. His countenance was quite disfigured and almost unrecognisable. His lips were white, and His hair stood on end. He ascended to the left of the grotto and up to a terrace upon which they were resting near one another supported on their arm, the back of one turned toward the breast of his neighbour. Exhausted with fatigue, sorrow, and anxiety under temptation, they had fallen asleep. Jesus went to them like a

man overwhelmed with sorrow whom terror drives to the company of his friends, and also like a faithful shepherd who, though himself trembling to the utmost, looks after his herd which he knows to be in danger, for He knew that they too were in anguish and temptation. All along this short distance, I saw that the frightful forms never left Him. When He found the Apostles sleeping, He clasped His hands and, sinking down by them from grief and exhaustion, He said: "Simon, you are sleeping?" At these words, they awoke and raised Him up. In His spiritual dereliction, He said: "What! Could you not watch one hour with Me?"

10) To exercise this immeasurable love for sinners, the Lord became man and the brother of sinners, that He might thus take upon Himself the punishment of all their guilt. He had indeed contemplated with anguish the immensity of that guilt and the greatness of the expiatory sufferings due to them, but at the same time He had offered Himself joyfully as a victim of expiation to the will of His Heavenly Father. Now, however, He beheld the sufferings, temptations, and wounds of the future Church, His Bride, which He had purchased at so dear a price, that of His own Blood, and He saw the ingratitude of man. Before the soul of the Lord there passed in review all the future sufferings of His Apostles, disciples, and friends, and the small number of the primitive Church. As her numbers increased, He saw heresies and schisms entering her fold, the sacrilegious crimes of all wicked priests against the most blessed sacrament, the scandals of the ages down to our own day and even to the end of the

world. The terror that I felt in beholding all this was so great, so dreadful, that my Heavenly Bridegroom appeared to me, and mercifully laying His hand on my breast, He said: "No one has ever before seen these things, and your heart would break with fright, did I not sustain it".

GLORY BE TO THE FATHER

Glory be to the Father and to the Son and to the Holy Spirit. As it was in the beginning is now, and ever shall be, world without end. Amen.

THE FATIMA PRAYER

O my Jesus, forgive us our sins, save us from the fires of hell, and lead all souls to Heaven, especially those in most need of Your Mercy.

The Scourging at the Pillar

THE FRUIT OF THIS MYSTERY:
PENANCE FOR OUR SINS.

PILATE CALLED OUT AGAIN: "WHICH OF THE TWO SHALL I release to you?" Thereupon arose from the whole forum and from all sides one unanimous shout: "Away with this Man! Give us Barabbas!" Pilate again cried: "But what shall I do with Jesus, the Christ, the King of the Jews?" With tumultuous violence, all yelled: "Crucify Him! Crucify Him!" Pilate asked for the third time: "Why, what evil has He done? I find not the least cause of death in Him. I will scourge Him and then let Him go". But the shout: "Crucify Him! Crucify

Him!" burst from the crowd like a roar from Hell, while the High Priests and Pharisees, frantic with rage, were vociferating violently. Then poor, irresolute Pilate freed the wretch Barabbas and condemned Jesus to be scourged! Pilate, the base, pusillanimous judge, had several times repeated the cowardly words: "I find no guilt in Him, therefore will I chastise Him and let Him go!" To which the Jews shouted no other response than, "Crucify Him! Crucify Him!" But Pilate, still hoping to carry out his first resolve not to condemn Jesus to death, commanded Him to be scourged after the manner of the Romans.

OUR FATHER

Our Father who art in heaven, hallowed be thy name. Thy kingdom come. Thy will be done, on earth as it is in heaven. Give us this day our daily bread; and forgive us our trespasses, as we forgive those who trespass against us; and lead us not into temptation, but deliver us from evil.

HAIL MARY XIO

Hail Mary full of Grace, the Lord is with thee. Blessed are thou among women and blessed is the fruit of thy womb Jesus. Holy Mary Mother of God, pray for us sinners now and at the hour of our death Amen.

MEDITATIONS

1) The executioners, striking and pushing Jesus with their short staves, led Him through the raging multitude on the forum to the whipping pillar, which stood in front of one of the halls that surrounded the great square to the north of Pilate's palace and not far from the guardhouse.

2) And now the executioners' servants came forward to meet Jesus, carrying their whips, rods, and cords, which they threw down near the pillar. There were six of them, swarthy men all somewhat shorter than Jesus, with coarse, crisp hair, to whom nature had denied a beard other than a thin, short growth like stubble. Their loins were girded and the rest of their clothing consisted of a jacket of leather, or some other wretched stuff, open at the sides, and covering the upper part of the body like a scapular. Their arms were naked, and their feet encased in tattered sandals. They were vile malefactors from the frontiers of Egypt who, as slaves and culprits, were here employed on buildings and canals. The most wicked, the most abject among them were always chosen for the punishment of criminals in the praetorium.

3) These barbarous men had often scourged poor offenders to death at this same pillar. There was something beastly, even devilish, in their appearance, and they were half-intoxicated. Although the Lord was offering no resistance whatever, yet they struck Him with their fists and ropes and with frantic rage dragged Him to the pillar, which stood

alone and did not serve as a support to any part of the building. It was not very high, for a tall man with outstretched arms could reach the top, which was provided with an iron ring. Toward the middle of it on one side were other rings, or hooks. It is impossible to express the barbarity with which those furious hounds outraged Jesus on that short walk to the pillar. They tore from Him Herod's mantle of derision, and almost threw the poor Saviour to the ground.

4) Jesus trembled and shuddered before the pillar. With His own hands, swollen and bloody from the tight cords, and in tremulous haste, He laid aside His garments, while the executioners struck and abused Him. He prayed and implored so touchingly and, for one instant, turned His head toward His most afflicted Mother, who was standing with the holy women in a corner of one of the porches around the square, not far from the scourging place. Turning to the pillar, as if to cover Himself by it, Jesus said: "Turn your eyes from Me!" I know not whether He said these words vocally or mentally, but I saw how Mary took them, for at the same moment, I beheld her turning away and sinking into the arms of the holy women who surrounded her, closely veiled.

5) And now Jesus clasped the pillar in His arms. The executioners, with horrible imprecations and barbarous pulling, fastened His sacred, upraised hands, by means of a wooden peg, behind the iron ring on top. In thus doing, they so stretched His whole body, that His feet, tightly bound below at the base, scarcely touched the ground. There stood the

Holy of Holies, divested of clothing, laden with untold anguish and ignominy, stretched upon the pillar of criminals, while two of the bloodhounds, with sanguinary rage, began to tear with their whips the sacred back from head to foot. The first rods, or scourges, that they used looked as if made of flexible white wood, or they might have been bunches of ox sinews, or strips of hard, white leather.

6) Our Lord and Saviour, the Son of God, true God and true Man, quivered and writhed like a poor worm under the strokes of the criminals' rods. He cried in a suppressed voice, and a clear, sweet-sounding wailing, like a loving prayer under excruciating torture, formed a touching accompaniment to the hissing strokes of His tormentors. Now and then the cries of the populace and the Pharisees mingled with those pitiful, holy, blessed, plaintive tones like frightful peals of thunder from an angry storm cloud.

7) The uproar was so great that, when he wanted to utter a few words, silence had to be enforced by the flourish of a trumpet. At such moments could be heard the strokes of the rods, the moans of Jesus, the blasphemy of the executioners, and the bleating of the Paschal lambs, which were being washed in the pool near the sheep gate to the east. After this first purification, that they might not again soil themselves, their jaws were muzzled and they were carried by their owners along the clean road to the Temple. They were then driven around toward the western side, where they were subjected to another ceremonial washing. The helpless bleat-

ing of the lambs had in it something indescribably touching. They were the only sounds in unison with the Saviour's sighs.

8) The Jewish mob kept at some distance, about the breadth of a street, from the place of scourging. Roman soldiers were standing here and there, but chiefly around the guardhouse. All kinds of loungers were loitering near the pillar itself, some in silence, others with expressions of contempt. I saw many of them suddenly roused to sympathy, and at such moments it seemed as if a sudden ray of light shot from Jesus to them. Just at this time, a numerous band of strangers on camels were riding past the forum. They gazed with fright and horror while some of the bystanders explained to them what was going on.

9) Christ's sacred blood was running down on the ground. He trembled and shuddered. Derision and mockery assailed Him on all sides. The last two scourgers struck Jesus with whips consisting of small chains, or straps, fastened to an iron handle, the ends furnished with iron points, or hooks. They tore off whole pieces of skin and flesh from His ribs. Oh, who can describe the awful barbarity of that spectacle! There was no longer a sound spot on the Lord's Body. He glanced, with eyes swimming in blood, at His torturers, suing for mercy; but they became only the more enraged. I saw the Blessed Virgin, during the scourging of our Redeemer, in a state of uninterrupted ecstasy. She saw and suffered in an indescribable manner all that her Son was enduring. Her punishment, her martyrdom, was as inconceivably great as

her most holy love. Low moans frequently burst from her lips, and her eyes were inflamed with weeping.

10) Jesus quivered in agony as, with bleeding wounds, He lay at the foot of the pillar. I saw just then some bold girls passing by. They paused in silence before Him, holding one another by the hand, and looked at Him in feminine disgust, which renewed the pain of all His wounds. He raised His bleeding head, and turned His sorrowful face in pity toward them. They passed on, while the executioners and soldiers laughed and shouted some scandalous expressions after them. Several times during the scourging I saw weeping angels around Jesus and, during the whole of that bitter, ignominious punishment that fell upon Him like a shower of hail, I heard Him offering His prayer to His Father for the sins of mankind. But now, as He lay in His own blood at the foot of the pillar, I saw an angel strengthening Him. It seemed as if the angel had given Him a luminous morsel to eat.

GLORY BE TO THE FATHER

Glory be to the Father and to the Son and to the Holy Spirit. As it was in the beginning is now, and ever shall be, world without end. Amen.

THE FATIMA PRAYER

O my Jesus, forgive us our sins, save us from the fires of hell, and lead all souls to Heaven, especially those in most need of Your Mercy.

The Crowning with Thorns

THE FRUIT OF THIS MYSTERY:
SUBMISSION TO THE KINGSHIP OF CHRIST.

THEY PUT UPON HIM THE CROWN OF THORNS. IT WAS two hands high, thick, and skilfully plaited, with a projecting edge on top. They laid it like a binder round His brow and fastened it tightly in the back, thus forming it into a crown. It was skilfully woven from thorn branches three fingers thick, the thorns of which grew straight out. In plaiting the crown, as many of them as possible had been designedly pressed inward.

OUR FATHER

Our Father who art in heaven, hallowed be thy name. Thy kingdom come. Thy will be done, on earth as it is in heaven. Give us this day our daily bread; and forgive us our trespasses, as we forgive those who trespass against us; and lead us not into temptation, but deliver us from evil.

HAIL MARY XIO

Hail Mary full of Grace, the Lord is with thee. Blessed are thou among women and blessed is the fruit of thy womb Jesus. Holy Mary Mother of God, pray for us sinners now and at the hour of our death Amen.

MEDITATIONS

1) The executioners again drew near and, pushing Jesus with their feet, bade Him rise, for they had not yet finished with the King. They struck at Him while He crept after His linen band, which the infamous wretches kicked with shouts of derision from side to side, so that Jesus, in this His dire necessity, had most painfully to crawl around the ground in His own blood like a worm trodden underfoot, in order to reach His girdle and with it cover His lacerated loins. Then with blows and kicks they forced Him to His tottering feet, but allowed Him no time to put on His robe, which they threw about Him with the sleeves over His shoulders. They

hurried Him to the guardhouse by a roundabout way, all along which He wiped the blood from His face with His robe.

2) The crowning and mocking of Jesus took place in the inner court of the guardhouse, which stood in the forum over the prisons. It was surrounded with pillars, and the entrance was open. There were about fifty low-lived wretches belonging to the army, jailer's servants, executioners, lads, slaves, and whipping servants, who took an active part in this maltreatment of Jesus. The mob at first crowded in eagerly, but was soon displaced by the thousand Roman soldiers who surrounded the building. They stood in rank and order, jeering and laughing, thereby giving to Jesus' tormentors new inducement to multiply His sufferings. Their jokes and laughter encouraged them as applause does the actor.

3) There was a hole in the middle of the court, and to this they had rolled the base of an old column, which may once have stood there. On that base they placed a low, round stool with an upright at the back by which to raise it, and maliciously covered it with sharp stones and potsherds.

4) Once more they tore Jesus' clothing from His wounded body, and threw over Him instead an old red military cloak tattered and so short that it did not reach to the knees. Shreds of yellow tassels hung on it here and there. It was kept in a corner of the executioners' room and used to throw around criminals after their scourging, either to dry the

blood or to turn them into derision. Now they dragged Jesus to the stool covered with stones and potsherds, and violently forced His wounded, naked body down upon them.

5) Then they put upon Him the crown of thorns and placed in Jesus' hand a thick reed with a tufted top. All this was done with mock solemnity, as if they were really crowning Him king. Then they snatched the reed from His hand and with it struck the crown violently, until His eyes filled with blood. They bent the knee before Him, stuck out their tongue at Him, struck and spat in His face, and cried out: "Hail, King of the Jews!" With shouts of mocking laughter, they upset Him along with the stool, in order to force Him violently down upon it again.

6) I am not able to repeat all the base inventions employed by those wretches to insult the poor Saviour. Ah! His thirst was horrible, for He was consumed with the fever of His wounds, the laceration caused by the inhuman scourging. He quivered. The flesh on His sides was in many places torn even to the ribs. His tongue contracted convulsively. Only the sacred Blood trickling down from His head laved, as it were in pity, His parched lips which hung languishingly open. Those horrible monsters, seeing this, turned His mouth into a receptacle for their own disgusting filth. Jesus underwent this maltreatment for about half an hour, during which time the cohort surrounding the praetorium in rank and order kept up an uninterrupted jeering and laughing.

7) And now they again led Jesus, the crown of thorns upon His head, the mock sceptre in His fettered hands, the purple mantle thrown around Him, into Pilate's palace. He was unrecognisable. on account of the blood that filled His eyes and ran down into His mouth and beard. His body, covered with swollen welts and wounds, resembled a cloth dipped in blood, and His gait was bowed down and tottering. The mantle was so short that He had to stoop in order to cover Himself with it, for at the crowning they had again torn off all His clothing. When He reached the lowest step of the flight that led up to Pilate, even that hard-hearted being was seized with a shudder of compassion and disgust.

8) Then Jesus was led forward by the executioners to the front of the balcony where Pilate was standing, so that He could be seen by all the people in the forum. Oh, what a terrible, heart-rending spectacle! Silence, awful and gloomy, fell upon the multitude as the inhumanly treated Jesus, the sacred, martyred figure of the Son of God, covered with blood and wounds, wearing the frightful crown of thorns, appeared and, from His eyes swimming in blood, cast a glance upon the surging crowd! Nearby stood Pilate, pointing to Him with his finger and crying to the Jews: "Behold the Man!"

9) While Jesus, the scarlet cloak of derision thrown around His lacerated body, His pierced head sinking under the weight of the thorny crown, His fettered hands holding the mock sceptre, was standing thus before Pilate's palace, in

infinite sadness and benignity, pain and love, like a bloody phantom, exposed to the raging cries of both priests and people. The Paschal lambs, whose gentle bleating was still mingling with the sanguinary shouts of the multitude, as if wishing to bear witness to the Silent Truth. Now it was that the true Paschal Lamb of God, the revealed though unrecognised Mystery of this holy day, fulfilled the Prophecies and stretched Himself in silence on the slaughtering bench.

10) Pilate ordered preparations to be made for pronouncing the sentence. His robes of ceremony were brought to him. A crown, in which sparkled a precious stone, was placed on Pilate's head, another mantle was thrown around him, and a staff was borne before him. Pilate, that iniquitous judge, who had in these last hours so frequently and publicly asserted the innocence of Jesus, now proclaimed that he found the sentence of the High Priests just, and ended with the words: "I also condemn Jesus of Nazareth, King of the Jews, to be nailed to the cross". Then he ordered the executioners to bring the cross. The most afflicted Mother of Jesus, the Son of God, on hearing Pilate's words became like one in a dying state, for now was the cruel, frightful, ignominious death of her holy and beloved Son and Saviour certain. John and the holy women took her away from the scene, that the blinded multitude might not render themselves still more guilty by jeering at the sorrow of the Mother of their Saviour. But Mary could not rest. She longed to visit every spot marked by Jesus' sufferings.

GLORY BE TO THE FATHER

Glory be to the Father and to the Son and to the Holy Spirit. As it was in the beginning is now, and ever shall be, world without end. Amen.

THE FATIMA PRAYER

O my Jesus, forgive us our sins, save us from the fires of hell, and lead all souls to Heaven, especially those in most need of Your Mercy.

The Carrying of the Cross

THE FRUIT OF THIS MYSTERY:
MORTIFICATION OF THE SENSES.

THE PROCESSION MOVED ONWARD. WITH BLOWS AND violent jerking at the cords that bound Him, Jesus was driven up the rough, uneven path between the city wall and Mount Calvary toward the north. At a spot where the winding path in its ascent turned toward the south, poor Jesus fell again. His tormentors beat Him and drove Him on more rudely than ever until He reached the top of the rock, the place of execution, when with the cross He fell heavily to the earth.

OUR FATHER

Our Father who art in heaven, hallowed be thy name. Thy kingdom come. Thy will be done, on earth as it is in heaven. Give us this day our daily bread; and forgive us our trespasses, as we forgive those who trespass against us; and lead us not into temptation, but deliver us from evil.

HAIL MARY XIO

Hail Mary full of Grace, the Lord is with thee. Blessed are thou among women and blessed is the fruit of thy womb Jesus. Holy Mary Mother of God, pray for us sinners now and at the hour of our death Amen.

MEDITATIONS

1) Here the High Priests parted from the true Paschal Lamb. They hurried to the Temple of stone, to slaughter and eat the type, while allowing its Realisation, the true Lamb of God, to be led to the altar of the Cross by infamous executioners. Here did the way divide—one road leading to the veiled, the other to the accomplished Sacrifice. They delivered the pure, expiating Paschal Lamb of God, whom they had outwardly mocked with their atrocious barbarity, whom they had striven to defile, to impure and inhuman executioners, while they themselves hastened to the stone Temple, there to sacrifice the lambs that had been washed, purified, and

blessed. They had, with timid care, provided against contracting outward legal impurity themselves, while sullying their soul with inward wickedness, which was boiling over in rage, envy, and scorn. "His blood be upon us and upon our children!" With these words they had fulfilled the ceremony, had laid the hand of the sacrifice upon the head of the victim. Here again, the road branched into two: the one to the Altar of the Law, the other to the Altar of Grace. The unjust sentence was pronounced at about ten o'clock in the morning according to our time.

2) A small band remained near the condemned. Twenty-eight armed Pharisees, among them those six furious enemies of Jesus who had assisted at His arrest on Mount Olivet, came on horseback to the forum in order to accompany the procession. The executioners led Jesus in to the centre. Several slaves, dragging the wood of the cross, entered through the gate on the western side, and threw it down noisily at His feet. As soon as the cross was thrown on the ground before Him, Jesus fell on His knees, put His arms around it, and kissed it three times while softly uttering a prayer of thanksgiving to His Heavenly Father for the Redemption of mankind now begun.

3) The executioners dragged Jesus up to a kneeling posture; and with difficulty and little help (and that of the most barbarous kind) He was forced to take the heavy beams upon His right shoulder and hold them fast with His right arm. I saw invisible angels helping Him, otherwise He would have

been unable to lift the cross from the ground. They jerked Him to His feet, and then fell upon His shoulder the whole weight of the cross, of that cross which, according to His own sacred words of Eternal Truth, we must carry after Him.

4) And now that blessed triumphal procession of the King of Kings, so ignominious upon earth, so glorious in the sight of Heaven, began. Two cords were tied to the end of the cross, and by them two of the executioners held it up, so that it could not be dragged on the ground. Around Jesus, though at some distance, walked the four executioners holding the cords fastened to the fetter-girdle that bound His waist. His mantle was tied up under His arms. Jesus, with the wood of the cross bound on His shoulder, reminded me in a striking manner of Isaac carrying the wood for his own sacrifice on the mountain.

5) The procession of the Crucifixion was headed by a trumpeter, who sounded his trumpet at every street corner and proclaimed the execution. Some paces behind him came a crowd of boys and other rude fellows, carrying drink, cords, nails, wedges, and baskets of tools of all kinds, while sturdy servant men bore poles, ladders, and the trunks belonging to the crosses of the thieves. The ladders consisted of mere poles, through which long wooden pegs were run. Then followed some of the mounted Pharisees, after whom came a lad bearing on his breast the inscription Pilate had written for the cross. The crown of thorns, which it was impossible to leave on during the carriage of the cross, was taken from

Christ's head and placed on the end of a pole, which this lad now carried over his shoulder.

6) Since the Last Supper of the preceding evening, without food, drink, and sleep, under continual ill-treatment that might of itself have ended in death, consumed by loss of blood, wounds, fever, thirst, and unutterable interior pain and horror, Jesus walked with tottering steps, His back bent low, His feet naked and bleeding. With His right hand He grasped the heavy load on His right shoulder, and with the left He wearily tried to raise the flowing garment constantly impeding His uncertain steps. The four executioners held at some distance the cords fastened to His fetter girdle. The two in front dragged Him forward, while the two behind urged Him on. In this way He was not sure of one step, and the tugging cords constantly prevented His lifting His robe. His hands were bruised and swollen from the cords that had tightly bound them, His face was covered with blood and swellings, His hair and beard were torn and matted with blood, the burden He carried and the fetters pressed the coarse woollen garment into the wounds of His body and the wool stuck fast to those that had been reopened by the tearing off of His clothes. Jeers and malicious words resounded on all sides. His lips moved in prayer, His glance was supplicating, forgiving, and suffering.

7) One of the men said to the bystanders: "Who is that woman in such distress?" And someone answered: "She is the Mother of the Galilean". When the miscreants heard this,

they jeered at the sorrowing Mother in words of scorn, pointed at her with their fingers; and one of the base wretches, snatching up the nails intended for the crucifixion, held them up mockingly before her face. Wringing her hands, she gazed upon Jesus and, in her anguish, leaned for support against one of the pillars of the gate. She was pale as a corpse, her lips livid. The Pharisees came riding forward, then came the boy with the inscription—and oh! a couple of steps behind him, the Son of God, her own Son, the Holy One, the Redeemer!

8) The executioners pulled Jesus forward with the ropes. His face was pale, wounded, and blood-stained, His beard pointed and matted with blood. From His sunken eyes full of blood He cast, from under the tangled and twisted thorns of His crown, frightful to behold, a look full of earnest tenderness upon His afflicted Mother, and for the second time tottered under the weight of the cross and sank on His hands and knees to the ground. The most sorrowful Mother, in vehemence of her love and anguish, saw neither soldiers nor executioners-saw only her beloved, suffering, maltreated Son. Wringing her hands, she sprang over the couple of steps between the gateway and the executioners in advance, and rushing to Jesus, fell on her knees with her arms around Him. I heard, but I know not whether spoken with the lips or in spirit, the words: "My Son!"—"My Mother!"

9) After going some distance up the broad street, the procession passed through a gateway in an old inner wall of the city.

In front of this gate was a wide open space at which three streets met. There was a large stepping stone here, over which Jesus staggered and fell, the cross by His side. He lay on the ground, leaning against the stone, unable to rise. Just at this instant, a crowd of well-dressed people came along on their way to the Temple. They cried out in compassion: "Alas! The poor creature is dying!" Confusion arose among the rabble, for they could not succeed in making Jesus rise. The Pharisees leading the procession cried out to the soldiers: "We shall not get Him to Calvary alive. You must call up someone to help Him carry the cross". Just then appeared, coming straight down the middle of the street, Simon of Cyrene, a pagan, followed by his three sons. The crowd was so great that he could not escape, and as soon as the soldiers saw by his dress that he was a poor pagan labourer, they laid hold on him and dragged him forward to help carry the Galilean's cross. He resisted and showed great unwillingness, but they forcibly constrained him.

10) Jesus again sank fainting. He did not fall to the ground, because Simon, resting the end of the cross upon the earth, drew nearer and supported His bowed form. The Lord leaned on him. At sight of His countenance so utterly wretched, the women raised a loud cry of sorrow and pity and, after the Jewish manner of showing compassion, extended toward Him kerchiefs with which to wipe off the perspiration. Jesus said some beautiful words to the women, among them, however, I remember these: "Your tears shall be rewarded, Henceforth, you shall tread another path",

GLORY BE TO THE FATHER

Glory be to the Father and to the Son and to the Holy Spirit. As it was in the beginning is now, and ever shall be, world without end. Amen.

THE FATIMA PRAYER

O my Jesus, forgive us our sins, save us from the fires of hell, and lead all souls to Heaven, especially those in most need of Your Mercy.

The Crucifixion of Our Lord

THE FRUIT OF THIS MYSTERY:
THE GRACE OF FINAL PERSEVERANCE.

FEAR AND CONSTERNATION FILLED JERUSALEM. FOG AND gloomy darkness hung over its streets. Many lay with covered heads in corners, striking their breasts. Others, standing on the roofs of the houses, gazed up at the sky and uttered lamentations. Animals were bellowing and hiding, birds were flying low and falling to the ground. The forum was deserted. The people had hurried to their homes. Anxiety and terror reached their height in the Temple. The slaughtering of the Paschal lamb had just begun when the darkness of night

suddenly fell upon Jerusalem. All were filled with consterna-
tion, while here and there broke forth loud cries of woe. The
High Priests did all they could to maintain peace and order.
Annas, terribly tormented, ran from corner to corner in his
desire to hide himself. Jesus, in unspeakable torture, endured
on the cross extreme abandonment and desolation of soul.
He prayed to His Heavenly Father in those passages of the
Psalms that were now being fulfilled in Himself. I saw around
Him angelic figures. He endured in infinite torment all that a
poor, crushed, tortured creature, in the greatest abandonment, without consolation human or divine, suffers when
faith, hope, and love stand alone in the desert of tribulation,
without prospect of return, without taste or sentiment,
without a ray of light, left there to live alone. No words can
express this pain. By this suffering Jesus gained for us the
strength, by uniting our abandonment to the merits of His
own upon the cross, victoriously to conquer at our last hour,
when all ties and relations with this life and mode of existence, with this world and its laws, cease; and when therefore
the ideas which we form in this life of the other world also
cease. He gained for us merit to I stand firm in our own last
struggle when we too shall feel ourselves entirely abandoned.

OUR FATHER

Our Father who art in heaven, hallowed be thy name. Thy
kingdom come. Thy will be done, on earth as it is in heaven.
Give us this day our daily bread; and forgive us our trespass-

es, as we forgive those who trespass against us; and lead us not into temptation, but deliver us from evil.

HAIL MARY X10

Hail Mary full of Grace, the Lord is with thee. Blessed are thou among women and blessed is the fruit of thy womb Jesus. Holy Mary Mother of God, pray for us sinners now and at the hour of our death Amen.

MEDITATIONS

1) It was about a quarter to twelve when Jesus, laden with the cross, was dragged into the place of execution, thrown on the ground, and Simon driven off. The executioners then pulled Jesus up by the cords, took the sections of the cross apart, and put them together again in proper form. Ah! How sad and miserable, what a terribly lacerated, pale and blood-stained figure was that of poor Jesus as He stood on that place of martyrdom! The executioners threw Him down again with words of mockery such as these: "We must take the measure of your throne for you, O King!" But Jesus laid Himself willingly upon the cross. Had it been possible for Him, in His state of exhaustion, to do it more quickly, they would have had no necessity to drag Him down.

2) Jesus was now stretched on the cross by the executioners, He had lain Himself upon it; but they pushed Him lower down into the hollow places, rudely drew His right hand to

the hole for the nail in the right arm of the cross, and tied His wrist fast. One knelt on His sacred breast and held the closing hand flat; another placed the long, thick nail, which had been filed to a sharp point, upon the palm of His sacred hand, and struck furious blows with the iron hammer. A sweet, clear, spasmodic cry of anguish broke from the Lord's lips, and His blood spurted out upon the arms of the executioners. The muscles and ligaments of the hand had been torn and, by the three edged nail, driven into the narrow hole.

3) The whole body of our Blessed Redeemer had been contracted by the violent stretching of the arms to the holes for the nails, and His knees were forcibly drawn up. They tied ropes around the right leg and, with horrible violence and terrible torture to Jesus, pulled the foot down to the block, and tied the leg fast with cords. Jesus' body was thus most horribly distended. His chest gave way with a cracking sound, and He moaned aloud: "O God! O God!" They had tied down His arms and His breast also that His hands might not be torn away from the nails. The abdomen was entirely displaced, and it seemed as if the ribs broke away from the breastbone. The suffering was horrible.

4) Jesus' moans were purely cries of pain. Mingled with them were uninterrupted prayers, passages from the Psalms and Prophecies, whose predictions He was now fulfilling. During the whole time of His bitter Passion and until the moment of death, He was engaged in this kind of prayer, and in the

uninterrupted fulfilment of the Prophecies. I heard all the passages He made use of and repeated them with Him, and when I say the Psalms, I always remember the verses that Jesus used. But now I am so crushed by the tortures of my Heavenly Bridegroom that I cannot recall them, I saw weeping angels hovering over Jesus during this terrible torture.

5) The position of the sun at the time of Jesus' Crucifixion showed it to be about a quarter past twelve, and at the moment the cross was lifted, the flourish of trumpets and trombones sounded from the Temple. It announced that the slaughter of the Paschal lambs had begun; and at the same time, with solemn foreboding, it broke in upon the shouts of mockery and the loud cries of lamentation around the true, slaughtered Lamb of God. Many a hard heart shuddered and thought of the Baptist's words: "Behold the Lamb of God, who has taken upon Himself the sins of the world!"

6) Along with those shouts of derision, there arose other sounds at that dreadful moment—sounds of love and compassion from His devout followers. In touching expressions of pity, the holiest voices on earth, that of His afflicted Mother, of the holy women, the beloved disciple, and all the pure of heart, saluted the "Eternal Word made Flesh" elevated upon the cross. Loving hands were anxiously stretched forth as if to help the Holy of Holies, the Bridegroom of souls, nailed alive to the cross, quivering on high in the hands of raging sinners. But when the upraised cross fell with a loud crash into the hole prepared for it, a moment of deep silence ensued. It

seemed as if a new feeling, one never before experienced, fell upon every heart. Hell itself felt with terror the shock of the falling cross and, with cries of rage and blasphemy, rose up again against the Lord in its instruments, the cruel executioners and Pharisees.

7) Among the poor souls and in Limbo, there arose the joy of anxious expectation about to be realised. They listened to that crash with longing hope. It sounded to them like the rap of the coming Victor at the door of Redemption. For the first time, the Holy Cross stood erect upon the earth, like another tree of life in Paradise, and from the Wounds of Jesus, enlarged by the shock, trickled four sacred streams down upon the earth, to wash away the curse resting upon it and to make it bear for Himself, the new Adam, fruits of salvation

8) While Jesus was being nailed to the cross, the thieves were still lying on the eastern side of the mount, their hands bound to the crosspiece fastened on their shoulders, and guards keeping watch over them. Both were suspected of the murder of a Jewish woman who, with her children, was travelling from Jerusalem to Joppa. The thieves looked up to Jesus, one praying, the other jeering. Both belonged to that band of robbers on the Egyptian frontiers from whom the Holy Family, on the flight to Egypt with the Child Jesus, received shelter for the night. Dismas was that leprous boy who, on Mary's advice, was washed by his mother in the water used for bathing the Child Jesus and instantly healed by it. The charity and protection which his mother, in spite

of her companions, then bestowed upon the Holy Family, was rewarded by that outward, symbolical purification, which received its realization at the time of the Crucifixion when, through the Blood of Jesus, her son was inwardly cleansed from sin. Dismas had gone to ruin and he knew not Jesus; still he was not utterly bad, and the patience of the Lord had touched him. Dismas, in deepest contrition and humble hope, raised his head to Jesus and said: "Lord, let me go to some place from where you may rescue me! Remember me when you come into your Kingdom!" Jesus replied to him: "Amen, I say to you, this day you shall be with Me in Paradise!"

9) The Blessed Virgin, overcome by maternal love, was in her heart fervently imploring Jesus to let her die with Him. At that moment, the Lord cast an earnest and compassionate glance down upon His Mother and, turning His eyes toward John, said to her: "Woman, behold, this is your son! He will be your son more truly than if you had given him birth". Then He praised John, and said: "He has always been innocent and full of simple faith". To John, He said: "Behold, this is your Mother!" and John reverently and like a filial son embraced beneath the cross of the dying Redeemer Jesus' Mother, who had now become his Mother also. Mary stood in her dignity as the Woman who was to crush the serpent's head. I felt that the purest, the humblest, the most obedient of creatures, she who said to the angel: "Behold the handmaid of the Lord! Be it done to me according to Thy word!"—she who had become the Mother of the Eternal

Word Incarnate, now that she understood from her dying Son that she was to be the spiritual Mother of another son, in the midst of her grief at parting and still humbly obedient, again pronounced, though in her heart, the words: "Behold the handmaid of the Lord! Be it done to me according to Thy word!" I felt that she took at that moment for her own children all the children of God, all the brethren of Jesus.

10) The hour of the Lord was now come. Jesus offered His misery, His poverty, His pains, His desolation for us miserable sinners, so that whoever is united with Jesus in the body of the Church must not despair at that last hour even if, light and consolation being withdrawn, he is left in darkness. Into this desert of interior night we are no longer necessitated to plunge alone and exposed to danger. Jesus has let down into the abyss of the bitter sea of desolation His own interior and exterior abandonment upon the cross, thus leaving the Christian not alone in the dereliction of death, when the light of heavenly consolation burns dim. For the Christian in that last hour of peril, there is no longer any dark and unknown region, any loneliness, any abandonment, any despair; for Jesus, the Light, the Truth, and the Way, blessed the dark way by traversing it Himself, and by planting His cross upon it, chased from it all that is frightful. The Blessed Virgin, supported in the arms of Mary Cleophas and Salome, was standing between Jesus and the cross of the good thief, her gaze fixed upon her dying Son. Jesus spoke: "It is consummated!" and raising His head He cried with a loud voice: "Father, into Your hands I commend My Spirit!" The sweet,

loud cry rang through Heaven and earth. Then He bowed His head and gave up the ghost. I saw His soul like a luminous phantom descending through the earth near the cross down to the sphere of Limbo. John and the holy women sank, face downward, prostrate on the earth.

GLORY BE TO THE FATHER

Glory be to the Father and to the Son and to the Holy Spirit. As it was in the beginning is now, and ever shall be, world without end. Amen.

THE FATIMA PRAYER

O my Jesus, forgive us our sins, save us from the fires of hell, and lead all souls to Heaven, especially those in most need of Your Mercy.

CONCLUDING PRAYERS

Upon concluding the recitation of the Holy Rosary, the following prayers are customary, but others too may be added according to one's devotion and preference.

HAIL, HOLY QUEEN

Hail Holy Queen, Mother of Mercy, Hail our life our sweetness and our hope. To thee do we cry, poor banished children of Eve, to thee do we send up our sighs, mourning and weeping in this vale of tears. Turn then most gracious Advocate thine eyes of mercy towards us and after this our exile, show unto us the blessed fruit of thy womb, Jesus. O clement, O loving, O sweet Virgin Mary. Pray for us O holy Mother of God, that we may be made worthy of the promises of Christ.

Let us pray

O God Whose only begotten son by His life death and resurrection has purchased for us the rewards of eternal life, grant we beseech Thee that meditating on these mysteries of the most Holy Rosary of the Blessed Virgin Mary we may both imitate what they contain and obtain what they promise, through the same Christ our Lord. Amen.

PRAYER TO SAINT MICHAEL THE ARCHANGEL

Holy Michael, the Archangel, defend us in the day of battle. Be our safeguard against the wickedness and snares of the devil. May God rebuke him, we humbly pray; and do thou, O Prince of the heavenly hosts, by the power of God thrust down into hell Satan and all the evil spirits who wander through the world seeking the ruin of souls. Amen.

MEMORARE

Remember, O most gracious Virgin Mary, that never was it known that anyone who fled to thy protection, implored thy help, or sought thine intercession was left unaided. Inspired by this confidence, I fly unto thee, O Virgin of virgins, my mother; to thee do I come, before thee I stand, sinful and sorrowful. O Mother of the Word Incarnate, despise not my petitions, but in thy mercy hear and answer me. Amen.

May the Divine Assistance remain always with us, and may the souls of the faithful departed, through the mercy of God rest in peace. Amen.

THE GLORIOUS MYSTERIES

❧

The Resurrection

THE FRUIT OF THIS MYSTERY:
HOLY JOY.

JOHN APPROACHED, FOLLOWED BY PETER. JOHN STOOD outside the entrance of the cave and stooped down to look, through the outer doors of the sepulchre, at the half-opened doors of the tomb, where he saw the linens lying. Then came Peter. He stepped down into the sepulchre and went to the tomb, in the centre of which he saw the winding sheet lying.

It was rolled together from both sides toward the middle, and the spices were wrapped in it. The bandages were folded around it, as women are accustomed to roll together such linens when putting them away. The linen that had covered the sacred face was lying to the right next to the wall. It too was folded. John now followed Peter to the tomb, saw the same things, and believed in the Resurrection. All that the Lord had said, all that was written in the Scriptures, was now clear to them. They had had only an imperfect comprehension of it before.

OUR FATHER

Our Father who art in heaven, hallowed be thy name. Thy kingdom come. Thy will be done, on earth as it is in heaven. Give us this day our daily bread; and forgive us our trespasses, as we forgive those who trespass against us; and lead us not into temptation, but deliver us from evil.

HAIL MARY XIO

Hail Mary full of Grace, the Lord is with thee. Blessed are thou among women and blessed is the fruit of thy womb Jesus. Holy Mary Mother of God, pray for us sinners now and at the hour of our death Amen.

MEDITATIONS

1) All was quiet and silent around the holy sepulchre. About seven guards were in front and around it, some sitting, others standing. The whole day long Cassius maintained his stand inside the sepulchre at the entrance of the tomb proper, leaving it scarcely for a few moments. He was still absorbed in recollection. He was in expectation of something that he knew was going to happen, for extraordinary grace and light had been vouchsafed to him. It was night; the lanterns before the tomb shed a dazzling light. I saw the Sacred Body wrapped in its winding sheet just as it had been laid on the stone couch. It was surrounded by a brilliant light and, since the burial, two angels had in rapt adoration guarded the sacred remains, one at the head, the other at the foot. They looked like priests. Their whole attitude, their arms crossed on their breast, reminded me of the cherubim on the Ark of the Covenant, excepting that they had no wings. The whole tomb, and especially the resting place of the Lord, reminded me in a striking manner of the Ark of the Covenant at different periods of its history. The light and the presence of the angels may have been in some degree visible to Cassius, and it may have been on that account that he stood gazing so fixedly at the closed doors of the tomb, like one adoring the Most Blessed Sacrament.

2) The blessed soul of Jesus in dazzling splendour, between two warrior angels and surrounded by a multitude of re-

splendent figures, came floating down through the rocky roof of the tomb upon the sacred body. It seemed to incline over it and melt, as it were, into one with it. I saw the sacred limbs moving beneath the swathing bands, and the dazzling, living body of the Lord with His soul and His Divinity coming forth from the side of the winding sheet as if from the wounded Side. The sight reminded me of Eve coming forth from Adam's side. The whole place was resplendent with light and glory.

3) Four of the guards had gone to the city to get something; the three others fell to the ground unconscious. They ascribed the shock to an earthquake but knew nothing of the cause. Cassius, however, was very much agitated and frightened, for he had a clear view of what had happened without fully understanding it. He kept to his post, and with great devotion awaited what would next take place. Meanwhile the absent soldiers returned. The earth trembled, and an angel in warrior garb shot like lightning from Heaven down to the tomb, rolled the stone to one side, and seated himself upon it. The trembling of the earth was so great that the lanterns swung from side to side, and the flames flashed around. The guards fell stunned to the ground and lay there stiff and contorted, as if dead. Cassius saw indeed the glory that environed the holy sepulchre, the rolling away of the stone by the angel, and his seating himself upon it, but he did not see the risen Saviour Himself. He recovered himself quickly, stepped to the stone couch, felt among the empty linens, and left the sepulchre, outside of which, full of eager desire, he

waited awhile, hoping to become the witness of a new and wonderful apparition.

4) I saw the risen Lord appearing to His Blessed Mother on Mount Calvary. He was transcendently beautiful and glorious, His manner full of earnestness. His garment, which was like a white mantle thrown about His limbs, floated in the breeze behind Him as He walked. It glistened blue and white, like smoke curling in the sunshine. His wounds were very large and sparkling; in those of His hands, one could easily insert a finger. The lips of the wounds formed the sides of an equilateral triangle which met, as it were, in the centre. of a circle, and from the palm of the hand shot rays of light toward the fingers. The souls of the early Patriarchs bowed low before the Blessed Mother, to whom Jesus said something about seeing her again. He showed her His wounds, and when she fell on her knees to kiss His feet, He grasped her hand, raised her up, and disappeared.

5) When, as they approached, the holy women noticed the lanterns of the guard and the soldiers lying around, they became frightened, and went a short distance past the garden toward Golgotha. Magdalen, however, forgetful of danger, hurried into the garden. Salome followed her at some distance, and the other two waited outside. The whole place was resplendent with light, and an angel was sitting at the right of the tomb. Magdalen was exceedingly troubled. When with beating hearts the women entered the sepulchre and drew near the holy tomb, they beheld standing before them the

two angels of the tomb in priestly robes, white and shining. The women pressed close to one another in terror and, covering their faces with their hands, bowed tremblingly almost to the ground. One of the angels addressed them. They must not fear, he said, nor must they look for the Crucified here. He was alive, He had arisen, He was no longer among the dead. Then the angel pointed out to them the empty tomb, and ordered them to tell the disciples what they had seen and heard, and that Jesus would go before them into Galilee.

6) Magdalen reached the Coenaculum like one beside herself, and knocked violently at the door. Some of the disciples were still asleep on their couches around the walls, while several others had risen and were talking together. Peter and John opened the door. Magdalen, without entering, merely uttered the words: "They have taken the Lord from the tomb! We don't know where"—and ran back in great haste to the garden of the sepulchre. Peter and John followed her, but John outstripped Peter.

7) Magdalen was quite wet with dew when she again reached the garden and ran to the tomb, her mantle had slipped from her head down on her shoulders, and her long hair had fallen around loose. As she was alone, she was afraid to enter the sepulchre at once, so she waited out on the step at the entrance. She stooped down, trying to see through the low doors into the cave and even as far as the stone couch. Her long hair fell forward as she stooped, and she was trying to

keep it back with her hands, when she saw the two angels in white priestly garments sitting at the head and the foot of the tomb, and heard the words: "Woman, why are you crying?" She replied loudly in her grief: "They have taken my Lord away! I don't know where they have laid Him!" Saying this and seeing nothing but the linens, she turned weeping, like one seeking something, and as if she must find Him. She had a dim presentiment that Jesus was near, and even the apparition of the angels could not turn her from her one idea. She did not appear conscious of the fact that it was an angel that spoke to her. She thought only of Jesus; her only thought was: "Jesus is not here! Where is Jesus?"

8) About ten steps from the sepulchre and toward the east, where the garden rose in the direction of the city, she spied in the grey light of dawn, standing among the bushes behind a palm tree, a figure clothed in a long, white garment. Rushing toward it, she heard once more the words: "Woman, why are you crying? Who are you looking for?" She thought it was the gardener. The apparition was not resplendent. It looked like a person clad in long, white garments and seen at twilight. At the words: "Who are you looking for?" Magdalen at once answered: "Sir, if you have taken Him from here, show me where you have laid Him and I will take Him away! "She glanced around, as if to see whether he had not laid Him some place near. Then Jesus, in His well-known voice, said: "Mary!" Recognizing the voice, and forgetting the crucifixion, death, and burial now that He was alive, she turned quickly and, as once before, exclaimed: "Rabboni!" ("Mas-

ter'). She fell on her knees before Him and stretched out her arms toward His feet. But Jesus raised His hand to keep her off, saying: "Do not touch Me, for I am not yet ascended to My Father. But go to My brethren, and say to them: I ascend to My Father and to your Father, to My God and to your God". Magdalen seemed possessed of the idea that Jesus was alive just as He was before, and that everything was as it used to be. I understood by those words that the first fruits of joy belong to God. It was as if Jesus had said that Magdalen should recollect herself and thank God for the mystery of Redemption just accomplished and His conquest over death.

9) Four of the soldiers returned from the tomb and went directly to Pilate with the report, Pilate heard every detail with secret terror but, letting nothing appear, sent them to Annas and Caiaphas. Annas became like one possessed. He was obliged to be confined, and he never again appeared in public. Caiaphas became like a madman devoured by secret rage. The four soldiers were seized and imprisoned. Jesus' enemies spread the report that His body had been stolen by the disciples; and the Pharisees, Sadducees, and Herodians caused the lie to be everywhere propagated, to be published in every synagogue in the whole world, accompanying it with slanderous abuse of Jesus. Their lies profited them little, for after Jesus' Resurrection, many souls of holy deceased Jews appeared here and there to those of their descendants still susceptible of grace and holy impressions, and frightened their hearts to conversion. To many of the disciples also who, shaken in faith and disheartened, were dispersed throughout

the country, similar apparitions appeared to console and strengthen them in faith.

10) On the evening of the same day, many of the disciples and all the Apostles assembled in the hall of the Last Supper, excepting Thomas who was in absolute retirement, the doors were closed. The meal was conducted with ceremony. The guests prayed standing and ate lying, while Peter and John taught. This was like the first catechetical instruction after Jesus' death. I saw all present radiant with joyful emotion, and glancing in the same direction. Jesus came in through the closed doors. He was robed in a long white garment simply girded. They did not appear to be really conscious of His approach until He passed through the circles and stood in their midst under the lamp. Then they became very much amazed and agitated. He showed them His hands and feet and, opening His garment, disclosed the Wound in His side. He spoke to them and, seeing that they were very much terrified, He asked for something to eat. I saw rays of light proceeding from His mouth. The Apostles and disciples were as if completely ravished.

GLORY BE TO THE FATHER

Glory be to the Father and to the Son and to the Holy Spirit. As it was in the beginning is now, and ever shall be, world without end. Amen.

THE FATIMA PRAYER

O my Jesus, forgive us our sins, save us from the fires of hell, and lead all souls to Heaven, especially those in most need of Your Mercy.

The Ascension

THE FRUIT OF THIS MYSTERY:
TRUST IN THE PROMISES OF THE LORD.

AFTER SOME MOMENTS, WHEN THE SPLENDOUR BEGAN
to diminish, the whole assembly in deep silence—their souls

swayed by varying emotions—gazed fixedly up at the brightness, which continued visible for a long time, I saw two figures appear in this light. They were clothed in long white garments, and each held a staff in one hand. They looked like Prophets. They addressed the multitude, their voices like trumpets resounding loud and clear. It seemed to me that they could surely be heard in Jerusalem. They made no motion, stood perfectly still, and said: "Men of Galilee, why are you standing, looking up to Heaven? This Jesus who is taken up from you into Heaven shall return as you have seen Him go". After these words the figures vanished. The brightness remained for a while longer and then disappeared like daylight retiring before the darkness of night. The disciples were quite out of themselves, for they now comprehended what had happened to them. Many, stunned by grief and amazement, fell to the earth. When the glare had entirely died away, they arose again, and the others gathered around them. They formed groups, the Blessed Virgin stepped forward, and so they stood for some time longer recovering themselves, talking together, and gazing upward. At last, the Apostles and disciples went back to the house of the Last Supper, and the Blessed Virgin followed. Some were weeping like children that refuse to be comforted, others were lost in thought. The Blessed Virgin, Peter, and John were very calm and full of consolation. I saw, however, some among the different groups who remained unmoved, unbelieving, and full of doubts. They withdrew from the rest.

OUR FATHER

Our Father who art in heaven, hallowed be thy name. Thy kingdom come. Thy will be done, on earth as it is in heaven. Give us this day our daily bread; and forgive us our trespasses, as we forgive those who trespass against us; and lead us not into temptation, but deliver us from evil.

HAIL MARY XIO

Hail Mary full of Grace, the Lord is with thee. Blessed are thou among women and blessed is the fruit of thy womb Jesus. Holy Mary Mother of God, pray for us sinners now and at the hour of our death Amen.

MEDITATIONS

1) At dawn of day Jesus left the house of the Last Supper with The Eleven. The Blessed Virgin followed them closely; the disciples, at some little distance. They passed through the streets of Jerusalem where all was quiet, the inhabitants still buried in sleep. At each moment the Lord became more earnest, more rapid in speech and action. On the preceding evening He appeared to me much more sympathetic in His words to His followers. I recognised the route that they took as that of the Palm Sunday procession. I saw that Jesus went with them over all the paths trodden by Him during His Passion, in order to inspire them by His teachings and ad-

monitions with a lively appreciation of the fulfilment of the Promise. In every place in which some scene of His Passion had been enacted, He paused a moment to instruct them upon the accomplishment of the words of the Prophets, upon the Promises, and to explain the symbolical relation of the place to the same.

2) Jesus paused to teach and comfort the little flock. Meanwhile, day dawned brightly; their hearts grew lighter, and they even began to think that Jesus would still remain with them.

3) New crowds of believers arrived, but I saw no women among them. Jesus again took the road that led to Mount Calvary and the Holy Sepulchre, but He did not follow it up to those points; He turned off and went around the city to the Mount of Olives. Some of the places on these roads consecrated to prayer and sanctified by Jesus' teaching, and which had been laid waste or hedged in by the Jews, were now restored by the disciples.

4) Jesus paused awhile with the crowd in an exceedingly cool and lovely spot covered with beautiful long grass, I was surprised to see that it was nowhere trodden down. The multitude that here surrounded Jesus was so great that I could no longer count them. Jesus spoke to them a very long time, like one who is about closing his discourse and coming to a conclusion. His hearers divined that the hour of parting

was near, and yet they had no idea that the time still intervening was to be so short.

5) The sun was already high, was already far above the horizon. I know not whether I express it rightly, for in that country it seems to me the sun is not so high as it is here. It always appears to me as if it were nearer to one. I do not see it as here, rising like a small globe. It shines there with far more brilliancy. Its rays are, on the whole, not so fine. They often look like a broad pathway of light, Jesus and His followers stayed here for an hour. By this time the people in Jerusalem were all on the alert, amazed at the crowds of people they descried around Mount Olivet. Out of the city, too, crowds were pouring in bands. They consisted of all that had gone out to meet Jesus on Palm Sunday. The narrow roads were soon thronged.

6) The Lord went only to Gethsemane and from the Garden of Olives up to the summit of the mount. He did not set foot upon the path on which He had been arrested. The crowd followed as in a procession, ascending by the different paths that encircled the mount. Many even pressed through the fences and garden hedges. Jesus at each instant shone more brightly and His motions became more rapid. The disciples hastened after Him, but it was impossible to overtake Him. When He reached the top of the mountain, He was resplendent as a beam of white sunlight. A shining circle, glancing in all the colours of the rainbow, fell from Heaven around Him.

7) The pressing crowd stood in a wide circle outside, as if blending with it. Jesus Himself shone still more brightly than the glory about Him. He laid the left hand on His breast and, raising the right, turned slowly around, blessing the whole world. The crowd stood motionless. I saw all receive the benediction. Jesus did not impart it with the flat, open hand, like the rabbis, but like the Christian Bishops. With great joy I felt His blessing of the whole world.

8) And now the rays of light from above united with the glory emanating from Jesus, and I saw Him disappearing, dissolving as it were in the light from Heaven, vanishing as He rose. I lost sight of His head first. It appeared as if one sun was lost in another, as if one flame entered another, as if a spark floated into a flame. It was as if one were gazing into the full midday splendours of the sun, though this light was whiter and clearer. Full day compared with this would be dark. First, I lost sight of Jesus' head, then His whole person, and lastly His feet, radiant with light, disappeared in the celestial glory. I saw innumerable souls from all sides going into that light and vanishing on high with the Lord. I cannot say that I saw Him becoming apparently smaller and smaller like something flying up in the air, for He disappeared as it were in a cloud of light.

9) Out of that cloud, something like dew, like a shower of light fell upon all below, and when they could no longer endure the splendour, they were seized with amazement and terror. The Apostles and disciples, who were nearest to Jesus,

were blinded by the dazzling glare. They were forced to lower their eyes, while many cast themselves prostrate on their faces. The Blessed Virgin was standing close behind them and gazing calmly straight ahead.

10) On the top of Mount Olivet, from which Jesus ascended, there was a level rock. On it He stood addressing the multitude before He blessed them and the cloud of light received Him. His footsteps remained impressed on the stone, and on another the mark of one hand of the Blessed Virgin. It was past noon before the crowd entirely dispersed. The Apostles and disciples now felt themselves alone. They were at first restless and like people forsaken. But by the soothing presence of the Blessed Virgin they were comforted, and putting entire confidence in Jesus' words that she would be to them a Mediatrix, a mother, and an advocate, they regained peace of soul.

GLORY BE TO THE FATHER

Glory be to the Father and to the Son and to the Holy Spirit. As it was in the beginning is now, and ever shall be, world without end. Amen.

THE FATIMA PRAYER

O my Jesus, forgive us our sins, save us from the fires of hell, and lead all souls to Heaven, especially those in most need of Your Mercy.

The Descent of the Holy Spirit

THE FRUIT OF THIS MYSTERY:
THE GIFT OF DIVINE WISDOM.

ON THE DAY OF PENTECOST, THE SACRED FIRE WAS
poured forth not only upon the Apostles and the Blessed

Virgin, but also upon the disciples and the women present in the antechamber, and thus the resplendent cloud gradually dissolved as if in a rain of light. The flames descended on each in different colours and in different degrees of intensity. After that effusion of heavenly light, a joyous courage pervaded the assembly. All were full of emotion, and as if intoxicated with joy and confidence.

OUR FATHER

Our Father who art in heaven, hallowed be thy name. Thy kingdom come. Thy will be done, on earth as it is in heaven. Give us this day our daily bread; and forgive us our trespasses, as we forgive those who trespass against us; and lead us not into temptation, but deliver us from evil.

HAIL MARY XIO

Hail Mary full of Grace, the Lord is with thee. Blessed are thou among women and blessed is the fruit of thy womb Jesus. Holy Mary Mother of God, pray for us sinners now and at the hour of our death Amen.

MEDITATIONS

1) On the following days I saw the Apostles always together and the Blessed Virgin with them in the house of the Last Supper. At the last repast of Jesus, and ever after, I saw Mary when at prayer and the breaking of bread always opposite

Peter, who now took the Lord's place in the prayer circle and at meals. I received at the time the impression that Mary now held a position of high importance among the Apostles, and that she was placed over the Church. The Apostles kept themselves very much aloof. I saw no one out of the great crowd of Jesus' followers going to them into the house of the Last Supper. They guarded more against persecution from the Jews and gave themselves up to more earnest and well regulated prayer than did the disciples dispersed in bands throughout the other apartments of the same house. The latter went in and out more freely. I saw many of them also very devoutly traversing the way of the Lord by night.

2) The whole interior of the Last Supper room was, on the eve of the feast of Pentecost, ornamented with green bushes in whose branches were placed vases of flowers. Garlands of green were looped from side to side. The Apostles stood in two rows turned toward Peter along either side of the hall, and from the side halls, the disciples ranged behind the Apostles took part in the hymns and prayers. When Peter broke and distributed the bread that he had previously blessed, first to the Blessed Virgin, then to the Apostles and disciples who stepped forward to receive it, they kissed his hand, the Blessed Virgin included. Besides the holy women, there were in the house of the Last Supper and its dependencies one hundred and twenty of Jesus' followers.

3) After midnight there arose a wonderful movement in all nature. It communicated itself to all present as they stood in

deep recollection, their arms crossed on their breast, near the pillars of the Supper Room and in the side halls, silently praying. Stillness pervaded the house, and silence reigned throughout the whole enclosure.

4) Toward morning I saw above the Mount of Olives a glittering white cloud of light coming down from Heaven and drawing near to the house. In the distance it appeared to me like a round ball borne along on a soft, warm breeze. But coming nearer, it looked larger and floated over the city like a luminous mass of fog until it stood above Sion and the house of the Last Supper. It seemed to contract and to shine with constantly increasing brightness, until at last with a rushing, roaring noise as of wind, it sank like a thunder cloud floating low in the atmosphere. I saw many Jews, who espied the cloud, hurrying in terror to the Temple. I myself experienced a childlike anxiety as to where I should hide if the stroke were to follow, for the whole thing was like a storm that had suddenly gathered, that instead of rising from the earth came down from Heaven, that was light instead of dark, that instead of thundering came down with a rushing wind. I felt that rushing motion. It was like a warm breeze full of power to refresh and invigorate.

5) The luminous cloud descended low over the house, and with the increasing sound, the light became brighter. I saw the house and its surroundings more clearly, while the Apostles, the disciples, and the women became more and more silent, more deeply recollected.

6) Afterwards there shot from the rushing cloud streams of white light down upon the house and its surroundings. The streams intersected one another in sevenfold rays, and below each intersection resolved into fine threads of light and fiery drops. The point at which the seven streams intersected was surrounded by a rainbow light, in which floated a luminous figure with outstretched wings, or rays of light that looked like wings, attached to the shoulders. In that same instant the whole house and its surroundings were penetrated through and through with light. The five-branched lamp no longer shone.

7) The assembled Faithful were ravished in ecstasy. Each involuntarily threw back his head and raised his eyes eagerly on high, while into the mouth of every one there flowed a stream of light like a burning tongue of fire. It looked as if they were breathing, as if they were eagerly drinking in the fire, and as if their ardent desire flamed forth from their mouth to meet the entering flame.

8) They gathered around the Blessed Virgin who was, I saw, the only one perfectly calm, the only one that retained a quiet, holy self-possession. The Apostles embraced one another and, urged by joyous confidence, exclaimed: "What were we? What are we now?" The holy women too embraced. The disciples in the side halls were similarly affected, and the Apostles hastened out to them. A new life full of joy, of confidence, and of courage had been infused into all. Their joy found vent in thanksgiving. They started to pray, gave

thanks and praised God with great emotion. The light meanwhile vanished. Peter delivered an instruction to the disciples, and sent several of them out to the inns of the Pentecost guests.

9) An extraordinary movement pervaded all nature. Good people were roused interiorly, while the wicked became timid, uneasy, and still more stiff-necked. Most of these strangers had been encamped here since the Pasch, because the distance from their homes rendered a journey to and fro between that feast and Pentecost altogether impracticable. They were become, by all that they had seen and heard, quite intimate and kindly disposed toward the disciples, so that the latter, intoxicated with joy, announced to them the Promise of the Holy Ghost as fulfilled. Then too did they become conscious of a change within their own souls and, at the summons of the disciples, they gathered around the Pool of Bethsaida. In the house of the Last Supper, Peter imposed hands on five of the Apostles who were to help to teach and baptise at the Pool of Bethsaida. They were James the Less, Bartholomew, Mathias, Thomas, and Jude Thaddeus. The last-named had a vision during his ordination. It seemed to him that he was clasping to his breast the Body of the Lord.

10) On the eighth day after Pentecost, Peter, vested in his episcopal mantle, celebrated Holy Mass. John and James the Less served him. I saw all the ceremonies performed just as Jesus had performed them at the institution of the Holy Eucharist: the Offertory, the pouring of wine into the chalice,

the washing of the fingers, and the Consecration. The communicants were kneeling, before them a narrow linen cloth, which two held on either side. I did not see the Faithful partake of the chalice.

GLORY BE TO THE FATHER

Glory be to the Father and to the Son and to the Holy Spirit. As it was in the beginning is now, and ever shall be, world without end. Amen.

THE FATIMA PRAYER

O my Jesus, forgive us our sins, save us from the fires of hell, and lead all souls to Heaven, especially those in most need of Your Mercy.

The Assumption of the Blessed Virgin

THE FRUIT OF THIS MYSTERY:
A TRUE DEVOTION TO THE BLESSED VIRGIN.

TWO DISCIPLES HELD BACK THE BUSHES FROM THE
entrance of Mary's tomb, they all went in and knelt in rever-

ent awe before the resting-place of the Blessed Virgin. John drew near to the light wicker coffin, which projected a little beyond the ledge of rock, undid the three grey bands which were round it and laid them aside. When the light of the torches shone into the coffin, they saw with awe and amazement the grave-clothes lying before them still wrapped round as before, but empty. About the face and breast they were undone; the wrappings of the arms lay slightly loosened, but not unwound. All came two by two into the narrow cave, and saw with amazement the empty grave-clothes lying before them. They looked up to Heaven with uplifted arms, weeping and praying, praising the Lord and His beloved transfigured Mother (their true dear Mother, too) like devoted children, uttering every kind of loving endearment as the spirit moved them. They must have remembered in their thoughts that cloud of light which they had seen from afar on their way home immediately after the burial, how it had sunk down upon the tomb and then soared upwards again.

OUR FATHER

Our Father who art in heaven, hallowed be thy name. Thy kingdom come. Thy will be done, on earth as it is in heaven. Give us this day our daily bread; and forgive us our trespasses, as we forgive those who trespass against us; and lead us not into temptation, but deliver us from evil.

HAIL MARY XIO

Hail Mary full of Grace, the Lord is with thee. Blessed are thou among women and blessed is the fruit of thy womb Jesus. Holy Mary Mother of God, pray for us sinners now and at the hour of our death Amen.

MEDITATIONS

1) Last night I had a great vision of the death of the Blessed Virgin, but have almost completely forgotten it all. The Blessed Virgin had reached the age of sixty-four years. After Our Lord's Ascension Mary lived for three years on Mount Sion, for three years in Bethany, and for nine years in Ephesus, where St. John took her soon after the Jews had set Lazarus and his sisters adrift upon the sea.

2) John had had a house built for the Blessed Virgin before he brought her here. Several Christian families and holy women had already settled here, some in caves in the earth or in the rocks, fitted out with light woodwork to make dwellings, and some in fragile huts or tents. They had come here to escape violent persecution. Their dwellings were like hermits' cells, for they used as their refuges what nature offered them. As a rule, they lived at a quarter of an hour's distance from each other. The whole settlement was like a scattered village. Mary's house was the only one built of stone.

3) I saw Mary becoming ever quieter and more meditative: she took hardly any nourishment. It was as if she were only here in appearance, as if her spirit had already passed beyond and her whole being was far away. In the last weeks before she died I sometimes saw her, weak and aged, being led about the house by her maidservant. Once I saw John come into the house, looking much older too, and very thin and haggard. Mary had a great longing to see Jerusalem again, and she was taken there by the Apostle John. On their arrival at Jerusalem in the dusk of the evening, before they went into the city, I saw them visiting the Mount of Olives, Calvary, the Holy Sepulchre, and all the holy places outside Jerusalem. She was inexpressibly sorrowful, constantly sighing, "Oh my Son, my Son". When she came to that door behind the palace where she had met Jesus sinking under the weight of the Cross, she too sank to the ground in a swoon, overcome by agonizing memories, and her companions thought she was dying.

4) Before the Ascension of her Son, the Holy Virgin had begged Him that she might not live for long in this vale of tears, and in response Jesus had told her in general what spiritual works she was to accomplish before her end on earth. He told her, too, that in answer to her prayers the Apostles and several disciples would be present at her death, and what she was to say to them and how she was to bless them. Now the Blessed Virgin prayed that the Apostles should come to her. I saw the call going forth to them in many different parts of the world. I saw all, the farthest as

well as the nearest, being summoned by visions to come to the Blessed Virgin. The indescribably long journeys made by the Apostles were not accomplished without miraculous assistance from the Lord. I think that they often travelled in a supernatural manner with out knowing it, for I often saw them passing through crowds of men apparently without anyone seeing them.

5) I saw the Holy Virgin lying on a low, very narrow couch in her little sleeping-alcove all hung with white, in the room behind and to the right of the hearth-place. Her head rested on a round cushion. She was very weak and pale, and seemed as though completely consumed with yearning. Her head and whole figure were wrapped in a long cloth; she was covered by a brown woollen blanket. I saw several women (five, I think) going into her room one after the other, and coming out again as though they were saying farewell to her. I now saw six of the Apostles already gathered here—Peter, Andrew, John, Thaddeus, Bartholomew, and Matthias—and also one of the seven deacons, Nicanor, who was always so helpful and anxious to be of service. Two more Apostles came in with girt-up garments like travellers. The newcomers tenderly embraced those who were already there, and I saw many of them weeping for joy and for sorrow, too—happy to see each other again and grieved that the occasion for their meeting was so sad.

6) Towards evening the Blessed Virgin realised that her end was approaching and therefore signified her desire, in accord-

ance with Jesus' Will, to bless and say farewell to the Apostles, disciples and women who were present. Her sleeping cell was opened on all sides, and she sat upright on her couch, shining white as if suffused with light. The Blessed Virgin, after praying, blessed each one by laying her crossed hands on their foreheads. She then once more spoke to them all, doing everything that Jesus had commanded her at Bethany. In the meantime the altar was set up and the Apostles vested themselves for the Holy Sacrifice of the Mass. During the Holy Sacrifice the Blessed Virgin sat upright on her couch in deep devotion. Peter, after he and the other Apostles had received Communion, brought Our Lady the Blessed Sacrament and administered Extreme Unction to her. The Apostles accompanied him in a solemn procession. The Blessed Virgin lay back on her pillows pale and still. Her gaze was directed intently upwards; she said no word to anyone and seemed in a state of perpetual ecstasy. She was radiant with longing; I could feel this longing, which was bearing her upwards—ah, my heart was longing to ascend with hers to God! As she received the Blessed Sacrament I saw a radiance pass into Mary, who sank back as though in ecstasy, and spoke no more. Mary's face was radiant with smiles as in her youth. Her eyes were raised towards Heaven in holy joy.

7) To my great joy I saw that Mary's soul, as it entered Heaven, was followed by a great number of souls released from Purgatory; and again today, on the anniversary, I saw many poor souls entering Heaven, amongst them some whom I knew. I was given the comforting assurance that every year,

on the day of Our Lady's death, many souls of those who have venerated her receive this reward. When I once more looked down to earth, I saw the Blessed Virgin's body lying on the couch. It was shining, her face was radiant, her eyes were closed and her arms crossed on her breast. The Apostles, disciples, and women knelt round it praying. As I saw all this there was a beautiful ringing in the air and a movement throughout the whole of nature like the one I had perceived on Christmas night. The Blessed Virgin died at the ninth hour, the same time as Our Lord.

8) Today I saw a number of women coming to prepare the body for burial. I saw the coffin lifted onto a bier and carried out of the house, six of the Apostles acted as bearers whilst the others knelt quietly, shedding many tears. It was already dusk, and four lights were carried on poles round the coffin. As the Apostles finished the work of laying the holy body in the rock hewn tomb, and had closed its door, night had fallen. All those present went in one by one and laid spices and flowers beside the body, kneeling down and offering up their prayers and their tears. Several of the Apostles and holy women remained the whole night in vigil, praying and singing in the little garden in front of the rock-tomb.

9) During this holy night I saw a broad shaft of light come down from Heaven to the rock, and I saw descending in it a triple-ringed glory of angels and spirits surrounding the appearance of Our Lord and of the shining soul of Mary. The appearance of Our Lord, whose wound-marks were stream-

ing with light, moved down in front of her soul. As this vision, becoming ever clearer, streamed down upon the rock, I saw a shining path opened and leading up to the heavenly Jerusalem. I saw Mary's soul, united to her transfigured body, rising out of the tomb far brighter and clearer, and ascending into the heavenly Jerusalem with Our Lord and with the whole glory. Thereupon all the radiance faded again, and the quiet starry sky covered the land. I do not know whether the Apostles and holy women praying before the tomb saw all this in the same manner, but I saw them looking upwards in adoration and amazement, or throwing themselves down full of awe with their faces to the ground. I saw, too, how several of those who were praying and singing by the Way of the Cross as they carried home the empty bier turned back with great reverence and devotion towards the light above the rock-tomb.

10) The next evening, I saw the Apostle Thomas and two companions, all girt up, arrive at the house of John and Mary and knocking to be let in. Oh, how distressed they were to learn that they had come too late! Thomas cried like a child when he heard of Mary's death. Thomas begged to be shown the tomb of the Blessed Virgin, so the Apostles kindled lights fastened to staves, and they all went out, passing along Mary's Way of the Cross, to the location of her tomb. When they came to the rock-tomb, they all threw themselves on their knees. The transfigured body of Mary was no longer on earth. John called to those outside the cave: "Come, see, and wonder, she is no longer here".

GLORY BE TO THE FATHER

Glory be to the Father and to the Son and to the Holy Spirit. As it was in the beginning is now, and ever shall be, world without end. Amen.

THE FATIMA PRAYER

O my Jesus, forgive us our sins, save us from the fires of hell, and lead all souls to Heaven, especially those in most need of Your Mercy.

The Coronation of the Blessed Virgin Mary and the Glory of all the Angels and Saints

THE FRUIT OF THIS MYSTERY:
DESIRE FOR PARADISE.

I SAW THROUGH THE SKY INTO THE HEAVENLY JERUSA-
lem. Two radiant clouds of light sank down, out of which

appeared the faces of many angels. Between these clouds a
path of light poured down upon Mary, and I saw a shining
mountain leading up from her into the heavenly Jerusalem.
She stretched out her arms towards it in infinite longing, and
I saw her body, all wrapped up, rise so high above her couch
that one could see right under it. I saw her soul leave her
body like a little figure of infinitely pure light, soaring with
outstretched arms up the shining mountain to Heaven. The
two angel-choirs in the clouds met beneath her soul and
separated it from her holy body, which in the moment of
separation sank back on the couch with arms crossed on the
breast. My gaze followed her soul and saw it enter the heavenly Jerusalem by that shining path and go up to the throne
of the most Holy Trinity. I saw many souls coming forward
to meet her in joy and reverence; amongst them I recognised
many patriarchs, as well as Joachim, Anna, Joseph, Elizabeth,
Zechariah, and John the Baptist. The Blessed Virgin soared
through them all to the Throne of God and of her Son,
whose wounds shone with a light transcending even the light
irradiating His whole Presence. He received her with His
Divine Love, and placed in her hands a sceptre with a gesture
towards the earth as though indicating the power which He
gave her.

OUR FATHER

Our Father who art in heaven, hallowed be thy name. Thy
kingdom come. Thy will be done, on earth as it is in heaven.
Give us this day our daily bread; and forgive us our trespass-

es, as we forgive those who trespass against us; and lead us not into temptation, but deliver us from evil.

HAIL MARY XIO

Hail Mary full of Grace, the Lord is with thee. Blessed are thou among women and blessed is the fruit of thy womb Jesus. Holy Mary Mother of God, pray for us sinners now and at the hour of our death Amen.

MEDITATIONS

1) The disciples left the Virgin's tomb and returned to the house by the Way of the Cross, praying and singing hymns. On their return they all went into Our Lady's room. John laid the grave-clothes reverently on the little table before the place where Our Lady used to pray. Thomas and the others prayed again at the place where she died. Peter went apart as if in spiritual meditation; perhaps he was making his preparation, for afterwards I saw the altar being set up before Our Lady's place of prayer where her cross stood, and I saw Peter holding a solemn service there, the others standing behind him in rows and praying and singing alternately. They made Mary's room in the house into a church. Mary's maidservant and a few women continued to live in the house; and two of the disciples, one of whom came from the shepherds beyond the Jordan, were left here to provide for the spiritual comfort of the faithful living in the neighbourhood.

2) Soon afterwards the Apostles separated to go their different ways. Bartholomew, Simon, Jude, Philip, and Matthew were the first to leave for the countries of their missions, after taking a moving farewell of the others. The others, except John, who stayed on for a while, went all together to Palestine before separating. All that I have described happened in stillness and quiet. There was secrecy but (unlike today) no fear. Persecution had not yet reached the stage of spies and informers, and there was nothing to disturb the serenity and peace.

3) I made a great journey with my guide, how I know not. We went over the city of Martyrs (Rome), then across the sea, and through a wilderness to a place where once stood the house of Anne and Mary, and here I left the earth. I saw innumerable cohorts of saints of endless variety, and yet in my soul, in my interior, they were all only one, all living and revelling in a life of joy, all interpenetrating and reflecting one another.

4) The place was like a boundless dome full of thrones, gardens, palaces, arches, flower gardens, and trees, with pathways sparkling like gold and precious stones. On high, in the centre, in infinite splendour was the throne of the Godhead. The Saints were grouped according to their spiritual relationship: the religious in their Orders higher or lower, according to their individual merits; the martyrs, according to their victories; and laity of all classes, according to their progress in the spiritual life, the efforts they had made to

sanctify themselves. All were ranged in admirable order in the palaces and gardens which were inexpressibly brilliant and lovely. I saw trees with little yellow luminous fruits.

5) They who were associated by similar efforts to sanctify themselves had aureoles of the same form, like a supernatural spiritual habit, and they were otherwise distinguished by emblems of victory, crowns, garlands and palms, and they were of all classes and nations. Among them I saw a priest of my acquaintance who said to me: "Your task is not yet finished!" I saw, too, legions of soldiers in Roman costume, and many people whom I knew, all singing together. I joined in a sweet song with them. I looked down on the earth which lay like a speck of land amid the waters; but, where I was, all was immense. Ah! life is so short, the end soon comes! One can gain so much—I must not be sad! Willingly and joyfully shall I accept all sufferings from my God!

6) All the Saints appeared with their various distinctive characteristics: many Bishops had little churches in their hands, because they had built churches; and others, croziers, as they had only discharged their duties as pastors. By them were trees laden with fruits. I saw the Saints in choirs according to their nature and strength, bringing materials to erect a throne, bringing all sorts of garlands, flowers, and decorations for it. All was done with indescribable order as is proper to a nature exempt from defect, sin, and death; all seemed to spring forth spontaneously.

7) I saw a church on earth and in it many whom I knew. Above were several other churches, higher and higher, like different stories, filled with angelic choirs; and higher still was the Blessed Virgin surrounded by the highest order, before the throne of the Most Holy Trinity. The grace of Jesus flows through Mary to the three Archangels, each of whom radiates three kinds of gifts upon three of the nine inferior choirs. These in their turn, pour them forth upon all nature and the whole human race. Here reigned indescribable order and activity; but below in the earthly church, all was drowsy and negligent to a degree.

8) I saw the Mother of God taken up from the low earthly Church by innumerable angels, borne, as it were, on a crown of five arches, on which she hovered over the altar. The Holy Trinity descended from the highest heavens and laid a crown on Mary's head. The choirs of angels and saints surrounded the altar at which the Apostles celebrated the Divine Service. These choirs were ranged like the side-chapels in a church.

9) At every step of the Blessed Redeemer during His passion, Mary had gathered the infinite merits that He acquired for us, and laid them up in her most holy and compassionate heart, that unique and venerable treasury of all the gifts of salvation, out of which and through which, according to the eternal degree of the triune God, every fruit and effect of the mystery of Redemption perfected in the fullness of time should be bestowed upon fallen man.

10) From the most pure blood of this most holy heart was formed by the Holy Ghost that Body which today was, from a thousand wounds, pouring forth Its precious Blood as the price of our Redemption. For nine months had Jesus dwelt under that heart full of grace. As a virgin inviolate had Mary brought Him forth, cared for Him, watched over Him, and nourished Him at her breast, in order to give Him over today for us to the most cruel death on the tree of the Cross. Just as the Eternal Father spared not His Only-Begotten Son, but delivered Him up for us, so the Blessed Mother, the Mother of God, spared not the Blessed Fruit of her womb, but consented that He, as the true Paschal Lamb, should be sacrificed for us upon the Cross. And so Mary is, in her Son and next to Him, the concurrent cause of our salvation, our Redemptrix, our Mediatrix and powerful Advocate with God, the Mother of grace and of mercy.

GLORY BE TO THE FATHER

Glory be to the Father and to the Son and to the Holy Spirit. As it was in the beginning is now, and ever shall be, world without end. Amen.

THE FATIMA PRAYER

O my Jesus, forgive us our sins, save us from the fires of hell, and lead all souls to Heaven, especially those in most need of Your Mercy.

CONCLUDING PRAYERS

Upon concluding the recitation of the Holy Rosary, the following prayers are customary, but others too may be added according to one's devotion and preference.

HAIL, HOLY QUEEN

Hail Holy Queen, Mother of Mercy, Hail our life our sweetness and our hope. To thee do we cry, poor banished children of Eve, to thee do we send up our sighs, mourning and weeping in this vale of tears. Turn then most gracious Advocate thine eyes of mercy towards us and after this our exile, show unto us the blessed fruit of thy womb, Jesus. O clement, O loving, O sweet Virgin Mary. Pray for us O holy Mother of God, that we may be made worthy of the promises of Christ.

Let us pray

O God Whose only begotten son by His life death and resurrection has purchased for us the rewards of eternal life, grant we beseech Thee that meditating on these mysteries of the most Holy Rosary of the Blessed Virgin Mary we may both imitate what they contain and obtain what they promise, through the same Christ our Lord. Amen.

PRAYER TO SAINT MICHAEL THE ARCHANGEL

Holy Michael, the Archangel, defend us in the day of battle. Be our safeguard against the wickedness and snares of the devil. May God rebuke him, we humbly pray; and do thou, O Prince of the heavenly hosts, by the power of God thrust down into hell Satan and all the evil spirits who wander through the world seeking the ruin of souls. Amen.

MEMORARE

Remember, O most gracious Virgin Mary, that never was it known that anyone who fled to thy protection, implored thy help, or sought thine intercession was left unaided. Inspired by this confidence, I fly unto thee, O Virgin of virgins, my mother; to thee do I come, before thee I stand, sinful and sorrowful. O Mother of the Word Incarnate, despise not my petitions, but in thy mercy hear and answer me. Amen.

May the Divine Assistance remain always with us, and may the souls of the faithful departed, through the mercy of God rest in peace. Amen.

THE MYSTERIES OF LIGHT

જ

The Baptism of Our Lord in the River Jordan

THE FRUIT OF THIS MYSTERY:
GRATITUDE FOR THE GIFT OF GRACE.

I SAW THAT THE ASPIRANTS FOR BAPTISM STOOD IN THE water up to the waist. John scooped up water in a shell and poured it on the head of the neophyte, while one of the baptised placed his hand upon the convert's shoulder. The upper part of the body of the neophytes was not entirely naked; a kind of white scarf was thrown around them, leaving only the shoulders bare. Near the pool was a hut into which they retired for unrobing and dressing. I never saw women baptised here. The Baptist wore a long, white garment during the ceremony. And now Jesus descended and stood in the water up to His breast. His left arm encircled the tree, His right hand was laid on His breast, and the loosened ends of the white, linen binder floated out on the water. On the southern side stood John, holding in his hand a shell with a perforated margin through which the water flowed in three streams. He stooped, filled the shell, and then poured the water in three streams over the head of the Lord, one on the back of the head, one in the middle, and the third over the forepart of the head and on the face. I do not now clearly remember John's words when baptising Jesus, but they were something like the following: "May Almighty God through the ministry of His cherubim and seraphim, pour out His blessing over You, with wisdom, understanding, and strength!" I cannot say for certain whether these last three words were really those that I heard; but I know that they were expressive of three gifts, for the mind, the soul, and the body respectively. In them was contained all that was needed to convert every creature, renewed in mind, in soul, and in body, to the Lord.

OUR FATHER

Our Father who art in heaven, hallowed be thy name. Thy kingdom come. Thy will be done, on earth as it is in heaven. Give us this day our daily bread; and forgive us our trespasses, as we forgive those who trespass against us; and lead us not into temptation, but deliver us from evil.

HAIL MARY X10

Hail Mary full of Grace, the Lord is with thee. Blessed are thou among women and blessed is the fruit of thy womb Jesus. Holy Mary Mother of God, pray for us sinners now and at the hour of our death Amen.

MEDITATIONS

1) During the three months immediately preceding the baptism of the Lord, John twice made the circuit of the country announcing Him who was to come. His progress was made with extraordinary vehemence. He marched on vigorously, his movements quick though unaccompanied by haste. His was no leisurely travelling like that of the Saviour. Where he had nothing to do, I saw him literally running from field to field. He entered houses and schools to teach, and gathered the people around him in the streets and public places. I saw the priests and elders here and there stopping him and

questioning his right to teach, but soon, astonished and full of wonder, they allowed him to proceed on his way.

2) The expression, "To prepare the way for the Lord", was not wholly figurative, for I saw John begin his mission by actually preparing the way and traversing the roads and different places over which Jesus and His disciples afterwards travelled. He cleared them of stones and briars, made paths, laid planks across brooks, cleaned the channels, dug wells and reservoirs, put up seats, resting places, and sheds to afford shade in the various places where later on the Lord rested, taught, and acted. Everywhere he was soon surrounded by a crowd whom he boldly and earnestly exhorted to penance, and to follow the Messiah of whom he announced himself the precursor. I often saw him pointing in the direction in which Jesus was passing at that moment, but yet I never saw him with Jesus.

3) But John saw the Lord always in spirit, for he was generally in the prophetic state. He saw Jesus as the accomplishment of his own mission, as the realisation of his own prophetic vocation. Jesus was not to John a contemporary, not a man like unto himself. He was to him the Redeemer of the world, the Son of God made man, the Eternal appearing in time, therefore he could in no way dream of associating with Him. John felt also that he himself was not like his fellow men, existing in time, living in the world and connected with it; for even in his mother's womb had the Hand of the Eternal touched him, and by the Holy Spirit had he in a way superior

to the relations of time, been brought into communication with his Redeemer. As a little boy he had been snatched from the world and, knowing nothing but what appertained to his Redeemer, had remained in the deepest solitude of the wilderness until, like one born anew, earnest, inspired, ardent, he went forth to begin his wonderful mission, unconcerned about aught else. Judea is now to him the desert; and as formerly he had had for companions the fountains, rocks, trees, and animals, as with them he had lived and communed, so now did he treat with men, with sinners, no thought of self arising in his mind. He sees, he knows, he speaks only Jesus. His word is: "He comes! Prepare the way! Do penance! Receive the baptism! Behold the Lamb of God who takes away the sins of the world!" In the desert, blameless and pure as a babe in the mother's womb, he comes forth from his solitude innocent and spotless as a child at the mother's breast. "He is pure as an angel", I heard the Lord say to the Apostles. "Never has impurity entered into his mouth, still less has an untruth or any other sin issued from it".

4) John delivered to his disciples at the Jordan a discourse upon the nearness of the Messiah's baptism. He told them that he had never seen Him, "But", said he, "I shall, as a proof of what I say, show you the place at which He will receive baptism. Behold, the waters of the Jordan will divide and from their midst an island will arise". At the same moment I beheld the waters of the river dividing and, on a level with its surface appeared a small, white island circular in shape. This happened at the spot over which the Children of

Israel had crossed the Jordan with the Ark of the Covenant and at which also Elias had divided the waters with his mantle. Wonder seized upon the beholders. They prayed and sang praises. The place upon which the Ark of the Covenant rested in the Jordan was the exact spot upon which the baptismal well of Jesus would be dug.

5) When John was informed of Jesus' approach, he roused himself and with new courage began to baptise in spite of the threats made by the Pharisees and the Herodians. Crowds came to John, chiefly those whom Jesus had exhorted to receive baptism, among them many publicans, but also Parmenas and his parents from Nazareth. When John spoke of the Messiah, saying that for Him he himself would soon make room, his words breathed so great humility as to cause real trouble to his disciples. The disciples whom Jesus had left in Nazareth also came to John. I saw them with him in his tent conversing about Jesus. John was so inflamed with ardent love for Jesus that he grew almost impatient at His not proclaiming Himself the Messiah openly and in unmistakable terms. When John baptised these disciples, he received the assurance of the nearness of the Messiah. He saw a cloud of light hovering over them, and had a vision of Jesus surrounded by all His disciples. From that moment, John became unspeakably joyous and expectant, constantly glancing into the distance, to see whether or not the Lord was yet in sight.

6) He had already baptised very many and it was drawing on to ten o'clock, when Jesus in His turn came down among the

aspirants to the pool of baptism. John bowed low before Him, saying: "I ought to be baptised by you, and you are coming to me?" Jesus answered: "Suffer it to be so now, for this is what righteousness demands, that you baptise Me and I be baptised by you". He said also: "You shall receive the baptism of the Holy Ghost and of blood". Then John begged Him to follow him to the island. Jesus replied that He would do so.

7) While Jesus ascended from the depths of the baptismal well, Andrew and Saturnin, who were standing to the right of the Baptist, threw about Him a large linen cloth with which He dried His Person. They then put on Him a long, white baptismal robe. After this Jesus stepped on a red triangular stone which lay to the right of the descent into the well, Andrew and Saturnin each laid one hand upon His shoulder, while John rested his upon His head. This part of the ceremony over, they were just about mounting the steps when the Voice of God came over Jesus, who was still standing alone and in prayer upon the stone. There came from Heaven a great, rushing wind like thunder. All trembled and looked up. A cloud of white light descended, and I saw over Jesus a winged figure of light as if flowing over Him like a stream. The heavens opened, I beheld an apparition of the Heavenly Father in the figure in which He is usually depicted and, in a voice of thunder, I heard the words: "This is My beloved Son in whom I am well pleased".

8) Jesus was perfectly transparent, entirely penetrated by light; one could scarcely look at Him. I saw angels around Him. But off at some distance on the waters of the Jordan, I saw Satan, a dark, black figure, as if in a cloud, and myriads of horrible black reptiles and vermin swarming around him. It was as if all the wickedness, all the sins, all the poison of the whole region took a visible form at the outpouring of the Holy Ghost, and fled into that dark figure as into their original source. The sight was abominable, but it served to heighten the effect of the indescribable splendour and joy and brilliancy spread over the Lord and the whole island.

9) The sacred baptismal well sparkled and seemed as a pool of living light. One could see the four stones that had once supported the Ark of the Covenant shining beneath the waters as if in exultation; and on the twelve around the well, those upon which the Levites had stood, appeared angels bending in adoration, for the Spirit of God had before all mankind rendered testimony to the living Foundation, to the precious, chosen Cornerstone of the Church around whom we as so many living stones, must build up a spiritual edifice, a holy priesthood, that thereby we may offer an acceptable, spiritual sacrifice to God through His beloved Son in whom He is well pleased.

10) John was seized by the Spirit and, pointing to Jesus, he cried out: "Behold the Lamb of God, who takes away the sins of the world!" Jesus passed, preceded and followed by His disciples in groups. It was early morning. The people crowd-

ed forward at the words of John, but Jesus had already disappeared. They called after Him in acclamations of praise, but He was out of hearing. When returned from their fruitless attempt to see Jesus, the people complained to John that Jesus had so many followers and that, as they had heard, His disciples had already begun to baptise. What, they asked, would be the outcome of all that. John made answer by repeating that he would soon resign his place to Jesus, since he was only a servant and precursor. These words were not at all acceptable to John's followers, who were somewhat jealous of Jesus' disciples.

GLORY BE TO THE FATHER

Glory be to the Father and to the Son and to the Holy Spirit. As it was in the beginning is now, and ever shall be, world without end. Amen.

THE FATIMA PRAYER

O my Jesus, forgive us our sins, save us from the fires of hell, and lead all souls to Heaven, especially those in most need of Your Mercy.

The Miracle at the
Wedding Feast of Cana

THE FRUIT OF THIS MYSTERY:
PATIENCE BEFORE THE ACCOMPLISHMENT OF GOD'S
HOLY DESIGNS.

JESUS AT THIS WEDDING FEAST WAS, AS IT WERE, IN THE
midst of His community for the first time. There it was that

He wrought that first miracle in their favour and for the confirmation of their faith. It is on that account that this miracle, the changing of water into wine is recorded as the first in His history; as that of the Last Supper, when His Apostles were staunch in the Faith, was the last. His disciples, His relatives, in a word, all present were now convinced of Jesus' power and dignity, as well as of His mission. All believed in Him. Faith at once took possession of every heart. All became better, more united, more interior. This same effect was produced in all that had drunk of the wine. At the close of the banquet, the bridegroom went to Jesus and spoke to Him very humbly in private. He told Him that he now felt himself dead to all carnal desires and that, if his bride would consent, he would embrace a life of continence. The bride also, having sought Jesus alone and expressed her wish to the same effect, Jesus called them both before Him. He spoke to them of marriage, of chastity so pleasing in the sight of God, and of the hundredfold fruit of the spirit. He referred to many of the Prophets and other holy persons who had lived in chastity, offering their bodies as a holocaust to the Heavenly Father. They had thus reclaimed many wandering souls, had won them to themselves as so many spiritual children, and had acquired a numerous and holy posterity.

OUR FATHER

Our Father who art in heaven, hallowed be thy name. Thy kingdom come. Thy will be done, on earth as it is in heaven. Give us this day our daily bread; and forgive us our trespass-

es, as we forgive those who trespass against us; and lead us not into temptation, but deliver us from evil.

HAIL MARY XIO

Hail Mary full of Grace, the Lord is with thee. Blessed are thou among women and blessed is the fruit of thy womb Jesus. Holy Mary Mother of God, pray for us sinners now and at the hour of our death Amen.

MEDITATIONS

1) When Jesus with His disciples arrived near Cana, He was most deferentially received by Mary, the bride's parents, the bridegroom, and others that had come out to meet Him. Jesus with His familiar disciples, among them the future Apostles, took up His abode in an isolated house belonging to the maternal aunt of the bridegroom. All the relatives of St. Anne and Joachim had come from around Galilee to Cana, in all over one hundred guests. Jesus Himself brought about twenty-five of His disciples with Him.

2) Long ago had Jesus, in His twelfth year at the children's feast held in the house of St. Anne upon His return from the Temple, addressed to the bridegroom words full of mysterious significance on the subject of bread and wine. He had told him that at some future day He would be present at his marriage. Jesus' participation in this marriage, like every other action of His earthly career, had, besides its high,

mysterious signification, its exterior, apparent, and ordinary motives.

3) More than once had Mary sent messengers to Jesus begging Him to be present at the wedding feast. The friends and relatives of the Holy Family, judging from a human view, were making such speeches as these: "Mary, the Mother of Jesus, is a lone widow. Jesus is roaming the country, caring little for her or His relatives" It was on this account, therefore, that Mary was anxious that her Son should honour His friends by His presence at the marriage. Jesus entered looked upon the present as a fitting opportunity to disabuse them of their erroneous ideas. He undertook also to supply one course of the feast, and so Mary went to Cana before the other guests and helped in the various preparations. Jesus had engaged to supply all the wine for the feast, wherefore it was that Mary so anxiously reminded Him that the wine failed.

4) Then I saw the wedding guests in a garden, the men and women separate, amusing themselves with conversation and games. The men reclined in circles on the ground. In the centre. were all kinds of fruit which, according to certain rules, they threw at one another. The thrower aimed at making it fall into certain holes or circles, while the others sought to prevent its doing so. I saw Jesus with cheerful gravity taking part in the game. Frequently He smilingly uttered a word of wisdom that made His hearers wonder. Deeply impressed, they received it in silence, the less quick to perceive its meaning asking for an explanation from their

neighbour. Jesus had the inner circle and decided the prizes, which He awarded with beautiful and sometimes quite astonishing remarks. The younger of the guests amused themselves by running and leaping over leafy festoons and heaps of fruit.

5) On the third day after Jesus' arrival, at about nine o'clock in the morning, the marriage ceremony was performed. The bride had been adorned by her bridesmaids. Her dress was something like that worn by the Mother of God at her espousals. The nuptial ceremony was performed by the priest in front of the synagogue. The rings exchanged by the young pair had been presented to the bridegroom by Mary after Jesus had blessed them for her.

6) The marriage ceremony was followed by the nuptial banquet. Jesus had engaged to supply the second course of the banquet as well as the wine, and for all this His Mother and Martha provided. This second course consisted of birds, fish, honey confections, fruits, and a kind of pastry which Veronica had brought with her. When it was all carried in and set on a side table, Jesus arose, gave the first cut to each dish, and then resumed His place at table. The dishes were served, but the wine failed. Jesus meanwhile was busy teaching. Now when the Blessed Virgin, who had provided for this part of the entertainment, saw that the wine failed, she went to Jesus and reminded Him that He had told her that He would see to the wine. Jesus, who was teaching of His Heav-

enly Father, replied: "Woman, do not worry, do not trouble yourself or me, My hour is not yet come".

7) Mary was the "Woman" who had brought forth Him whom now, as her Creator, she invokes on the occasion of the wine's failing. As the Creator, He will now give a proof of His high dignity. He will here show that He is the Son of God and not solely the Son of Mary. Later on, when dying upon the Cross, He again addressed His weeping Mother by the appellation of Woman, "Woman, behold your son!" thereby designating John. Jesus had promised His Mother that He would provide the wine. And here we see Mary beginning the role of Mediatrix that she has ever since continued. She places before Him the failure of the wine. But the wine that He was about to provide was more than ordinary wine; it was symbolical of that mystery by which He would one day change wine into His own Blood. The reply: "My hour has not yet come", contained three significations: first, the hour for supplying the promised wine; secondly, the hour for changing water into wine, thirdly, the hour for changing wine into His own Blood.

8) Mary's anxiety for the wedding guests was now entirely relieved. She had mentioned the matter to her Son, therefore she says confidently to the servants: "Do all that He shall tell you". In like manner does the Church, the Bride of Jesus, say to Him: "Lord, your children have no wine". And Jesus replies: "Church" (not Bride), "be not troubled, be not disquieted! My hour is not yet come". Then says the Church

to her priests: "Hearken to His words, obey all His commands, for He will always help you!"

9) Mary's words to Jesus had been uttered in a low tone, but Jesus' reply, as well as His command to draw water, was given in a loud voice. When the jugs filled with water had been placed, six in number, on the side table, Jesus went and blessed them. As He retook His place at the table, He called to a servant: "Draw some off now, and bring a drink to the steward!" When this latter had tasted the wine, he approached the bridegroom and said: "Every man at first serves good wine, and when men have had something to drink, then that which is worse. But you have kept the good wine until now".

10) Then the bridegroom and the bride's father drank of the wine, and great was their astonishment. The servants protested that they had drawn only water, and that the drinking vessels and glasses on the table had been filled with the same. And now the whole company drank. The miracle gave rise to no alarm or excitement; on the contrary, a spirit of silent awe and reverence fell upon them. Jesus taught much upon this miracle.

GLORY BE TO THE FATHER

Glory be to the Father and to the Son and to the Holy Spirit. As it was in the beginning is now, and ever shall be, world without end. Amen.

THE FATIMA PRAYER

O my Jesus, forgive us our sins, save us from the fires of hell, and lead all souls to Heaven, especially those in most need of Your Mercy.

The Proclamation of the Kingdom and the Call to Conversion

THE FRUIT OF THIS MYSTERY:
ZEAL FOR SOULS.

AFTER THE CLOSE OF THE SABBATH, JESUS WENT WITH his disciples into a little valley near the synagogue. It seemed intended for a promenade or a place of seclusion. There were trees in front of the entrance, as well as in the vale. The sons of Mary Cleophas, of Zebedee, and some others of the disciples were with Him. But Philip, who was hesitant and humble, hung behind, not certain as to whether he should or should not follow. Jesus, who was going on before, turned His head and, addressing Philip, said: "Follow Me!" at which words Philip went on joyously with the others. There were about twelve in the little band.

OUR FATHER

Our Father who art in heaven, hallowed be thy name. Thy kingdom come. Thy will be done, on earth as it is in heaven. Give us this day our daily bread; and forgive us our trespasses, as we forgive those who trespass against us; and lead us not into temptation, but deliver us from evil.

HAIL MARY XIO

Hail Mary full of Grace, the Lord is with thee. Blessed are thou among women and blessed is the fruit of thy womb Jesus. Holy Mary Mother of God, pray for us sinners now and at the hour of our death Amen.

MEDITATIONS

1) At the close of the feast, Jesus left Ono with twenty-one disciples and journeyed to Galilee. His way led through the region in which Jacob had owned a field, and among those shepherd houses, from one of which Joseph and Mary had been so harshly turned away on their journey to Bethlehem. He visited the occupants of the inn that had extended hospitality to the holy travellers, and instructed them; with those

of the inhospitable one, He stayed overnight and admonished them to be converted. The woman of the house was still alive, though on a sickbed. Jesus cured her.

2) Jairus had some time previously begged Jesus to cure his sick daughter, and Jesus had promised to do so, though not just then. Although his daughter was dead, Jairus now dispatched a messenger to meet Him and remind Him of His promise. Jesus sent His disciples on ahead after appointing a certain place where they should again meet Him, and He Himself accompanied Jairus' messenger back to him. When He entered the house of Jairus, the daughter lay wrapped in the winding-sheet ready for burial, her weeping friends around her. Jesus ordered the neighbours to be called in, and the winding-sheet and linens to be loosened. Then taking the dead girl by the hand, He commanded her to arise.

3) The girl arose, and stood before Him. She was about sixteen years old and not good. She had no love for her father, although he prized her above all things. He was charitable and pious, and shrank not from communication with the poor and despised. That was a source of vexation to his daughter. Jesus roused her from death both of soul and body. She reformed, and some time after joined the holy women. Jesus warned those present not to speak of the miracle they had witnessed. It was through the same desire of secrecy that He had not allowed the disciples to accompany Him.

4) Jesus taught in Jezrael and performed many miracles before a great concourse of people. All the disciples from Galilee were here assembled to meet Him. Johanna Chusa, who had come before from Jerusalem, had visited Magdalen at her castle of Magdala to persuade her to go with them to Jezrael in order to see, if not to hear, the wise, the admirable, the most eloquent, and most beautiful Jesus, of whom the whole country was full. Magdalen had yielded to the persuasions of the women and, surrounded by much vain display, accompanied them there. As she stood at the window of an inn gazing down into the street, Jesus and His disciples came walking by. He looked at her gravely as He passed with a glance that pierced her soul. An unusual feeling of confusion came over her. Violently agitated, she rushed from the inn and, impelled by an overpowering sense of her own misery, hid in a house wherein lepers and women afflicted with ailments found a refuge. Magdalen had fled to the house of the leprous through that feeling of intense humiliation roused in her soul by the glance of Jesus.

5) Numbers of sick and possessed were brought to Him from the country around. He cured them openly before all His disciples, and drove the devils out in presence of an ever-increasing crowd. Messengers came from Sidon begging Him to go back with them, but He put them off kindly until a future day. The crowd became so great that at the close of the Sabbath Jesus left Capharnaum with some of His disciples, and escaped into a mountainous district about an hour to the north of the city. It was situated between the lake and the

mouth of the Jordan, and was full of ravines. Into one of these He retired alone to pray.

6) When Jesus entered Bethulia, the possessed began to cry after Him in the streets. On arriving at the marketplace, He stood still near a teacher's chair and sent some of His disciples with directions to the superior of the synagogue to have the doors on all sides of the school opened. Others were sent from house to house to call the occupants to the instruction. The synagogue was surrounded by doors between the columns, and it was customary to throw them open when the crowd was exceptionally great. Jesus taught here of the tiny grain of wheat that must be cast into the earth. The Pharisees here did not indeed openly contradict, but they murmured, and Jesus knew that they did so, because they feared He would celebrate the Sabbath among them.

7) That night I again saw Jesus praying with outstretched arms, and again appearing on the Sea of Galilee to bear help in a storm. This time the distress was much greater, and many more vessels were in danger. I saw Jesus laying His hand on the helm without the helmsman seeing Him. The three rich youths of Nazareth who had once before vainly offered their petition to Him to be received as disciples came to Him again, reiterating their request. They almost knelt before Him, but He sent them away after pointing out certain conditions that had to be fulfilled before He would allow them to join His disciples. Jesus knew well that their views were entirely worldly, and that they could not under-

stand Him. They wanted to follow Him because they saw in Him a philosopher, a learned Rabbi. After a time spent in His school, they could, as they thought, shine with a more brilliant reputation and do honour to their city Nazareth. They were besides somewhat vexed at seeing Him giving the preference to the poor sons of Nazareth rather than to themselves.

8) Until far into the night I saw Jesus with the old Essenian, Eliud of Nazareth. The holy man looked as if he would soon die of old age. He was no longer able for much, indeed he was almost bedridden. Jesus leaned on His arm at the bedside and talked with him. Eliud was entirely absorbed in God.

9) On the Sabbath Jesus taught in the synagogue. The passages read from Holy Scripture referred to the journey through the Wilderness, the parcelling out of the Land of Canaan, and to something in Jeremiah. Jesus interpreted all as bearing reference to the nearness of the Kingdom of God. He spoke of the murmuring of the Children of Israel in the desert, saying that they would have taken a much shorter way to the Promised Land, had they kept the Commandments that God gave them on Sinai, but on account of their sins they were obliged to wander, and they that murmured died in the desert. And so, too, would they among His present hearers wander in the desert and die therein, if they murmured against the Kingdom that was now at hand and with it the final mercy of God. Their life had been an image of that wandering in the desert, but they should now go by the

shortest way to the promised Kingdom of God, which would be pointed out to them.

10) Magdalen with streaming hair and uttering loud lamentations, made her way through the crowd, cast herself at Jesus' feet, weeping and moaning, and asked if she might still hope for salvation. The Pharisees and disciples, scandalised at the sight, said to Jesus that He should no longer suffer this reprobate woman to create disturbance everywhere, that He should send her away once for all. But Jesus replied: "Let her weep and lament! You don't know what is passing in her"— and He turned to her with words of consolation. He told her to repent from her heart, to believe and to hope, for that she should soon find peace. She cried for pardon, confessed her numerous transgressions, and asked over and over: "Lord, is there still salvation for me?" Jesus forgave her sins, and she implored Him to save her from another relapse. He promised so to do, gave her His blessing, and spoke to her of the virtue of purity, also of His Mother, who was pure without stain. Jesus took Magdalen to rejoined the holy women, He said to them: "She has been a great sinner, but for all future time, she will be the model of penitents".

GLORY BE TO THE FATHER

Glory be to the Father and to the Son and to the Holy Spirit. As it was in the beginning is now, and ever shall be, world without end. Amen.

THE FATIMA PRAYER

O my Jesus, forgive us our sins, save us from the fires of hell, and lead all souls to Heaven, especially those in most need of Your Mercy.

The Transfiguration of the Lord on Mount Tabor

THE FRUIT OF THIS MYSTERY:
ADORATION BEFORE GOD INCARNATE.

JESUS TOLD THEM THAT HE HAD ALLOWED THEM TO
behold the Transfiguration of the Son of Man in order to

strengthen their faith, that they might not waver when they saw Him delivered for the sins of the world into the hands of evildoers, that they might not be scandalised when they witnessed His humiliation, and that they might at that time strengthen their weaker brethren. He again alluded to the faith of Peter who, enlightened by God, had been the first of His followers to penetrate the mystery of His Divinity, and He spoke of the rock upon which He was going to build His Church. Then they united again in prayer, and by the morning light descended the north-western side of the mountain.

OUR FATHER

Our Father who art in heaven, hallowed be thy name. Thy kingdom come. Thy will be done, on earth as it is in heaven. Give us this day our daily bread; and forgive us our trespasses, as we forgive those who trespass against us; and lead us not into temptation, but deliver us from evil.

HAIL MARY XIO

Hail Mary full of Grace, the Lord is with thee. Blessed are thou among women and blessed is the fruit of thy womb Jesus. Holy Mary Mother of God, pray for us sinners now and at the hour of our death Amen.

MEDITATIONS

1) Taking with Him Peter, John, and James the Greater, He proceeded up the mountain by a footpath. They spent nearly two hours in ascent, for Jesus paused frequently at the different caves and places made memorable by the sojourn of the Prophets. There He explained to them manifold mysteries and united with them in prayer.

2) They had no provisions, for Jesus had forbidden them to bring any, saying that they would be satisfied to overflowing. The view from the summit of the mountain extended far and wide. On it was a large open place surrounded by a wall and shade trees. The ground was covered with aromatic herbs and sweet-scented flowers.

3) Jesus here continued His instructions. His words were extraordinarily loving, like those of one inspired, and the disciples were wholly inebriated by them. In the beginning of His instruction, He had said that He would show them who He was, they should behold Him glorified, that they might not waver in faith when His enemies would mock and maltreat Him, when they should behold Him in death shorn of all glory.

4) The sun had set and it was dark, but the Apostles had not remarked the fact, so entrancing were Jesus' words and bearing. He became brighter and brighter, and apparitions of angelic spirits hovered around Him. Peter saw them, for he

interrupted Jesus with the question: "Master, what does this mean?" Jesus answered: "They serve Me!" Peter, quite out of himself, stretched forth his hands, exclaiming: "Master, are we not here? We will serve Thee in all things!"

5) The Apostles lay, ravished in ecstasy rather than in sleep, prostrate on their faces. Then I saw three shining figures approaching Jesus in the light. Their coming appeared perfectly natural. It was like that of one who steps from the darkness of night into a place brilliantly illuminated. Two of them appeared in a more definite form, a form more like the corporeal. They addressed Jesus and conversed with Him. They were Moses and Elias. The third apparition spoke no word. It was more ethereal, more spiritual. That was Malachi.

6) I heard Moses and Elias greet Jesus, and I heard Him speaking to them of His Passion and of Redemption. Their being together appeared perfectly simple and natural. Moses and Elias did not look aged nor decrepit as when they left the earth. They were, on the contrary, in the bloom of youth. Moses—taller, graver, and more majestic than Elias—had on his forehead something like two projecting bumps. He was clothed in a long garment. simplicity. He told Jesus how rejoiced he was to see Him who had led himself and his people out of Egypt, and who was now once more about to redeem them. He referred to the numerous types of the Saviour in his own time, and uttered deeply significant words upon the Paschal lamb and the Lamb of God.

7) Jesus spoke with them of all the sufferings He had endured up to the present, and of all that still awaited Him. He related the history of His passion in detail, point for point. Elias and Moses frequently expressed their emotion and joy. Their words were full of sympathy and consolation, of reverence for the Saviour, and of the uninterrupted praises of God. They constantly referred to the types of the mysteries of which Jesus was speaking, and praised God for having from all eternity dealt in mercy toward His people. But Malachi kept silence. The disciples raised their heads, gazed long upon the glory of Jesus, and beheld Moses, Elias, and Malachi. When in describing His passion Jesus came to His exaltation on the Cross, He extended His arms at the words: "So shall the Son of Man be lifted up!" His face was turned toward the south, He was entirely penetrated with light, and His robe flashed with a bluish white gleam. He, the Prophets, and the three Apostles—all were raised above the earth.

8) And now the Prophets separated from Jesus, Elias and Moses vanishing toward the east, Malachi westward into the darkness. Then Peter, ravished with joy, exclaimed: "Master, it is good for us to be here! Let us make here three tabernacles: one for You, one for Moses, and one for Elias!" Peter meant that they had need of no other Heaven, for where they were was so sweet and blessed. By the tabernacles, he meant places of rest and honour, the dwellings of the saints. He said this in the delirium of his joy, in his state of ecstasy, without knowing what he was saying.

9) When they had returned to their usual waking state, a cloud of white light descended upon them, like the morning dew floating over the meadows. I saw the heavens open above Jesus and the vision of the Most Holy Trinity, God the Father seated on a throne. He looked like an aged priest, and at His feet were crowds of angels and celestial figures. A stream of light descended upon Jesus, and the Apostles heard above them, like a sweet, gentle sighing, a voice pronouncing the words: "This is My beloved Son in whom I am well pleased. Listen to Him!" Fear and trembling fell upon them. Overcome by the sense of their own human weakness and the glory they beheld, they cast themselves face downward on the earth. They trembled in the presence of Jesus, in whose favour they had just heard the testimony of His Heavenly Father.

10) Jesus went to them, touched them, and said: "Arise, Do not be afraid!" They arose, and beheld Jesus alone. It was now approaching three in the morning. The grey dawn was glimmering in the heavens and the damp vapours were hanging over the country around the foot of the mountain. The Apostles were silent through fear of what they had seen.

GLORY BE TO THE FATHER

Glory be to the Father and to the Son and to the Holy Spirit. As it was in the beginning is now, and ever shall be, world without end. Amen.

THE FATIMA PRAYER

O my Jesus, forgive us our sins, save us from the fires of hell, and lead all souls to Heaven, especially those in most need of Your Mercy.

The Institution of the Holy Eucharist

THE FRUIT OF THIS MYSTERY:
FAITH IN THE REAL PRESENCE OF CHRIST IN THE
MOST BLESSED SACRAMENT.

THE BREAKING AND DISTRIBUTING OF BREAD AND drinking out of the same cup were customary in olden times at feasts of welcome and farewell. They were used as signs of brotherly love and friendship. I think there must be something about it in the Scriptures. Today Jesus elevated this custom to the dignity of the Most Holy Sacrament, for until now it was only a typical ceremony. Jesus' place was between Peter and John. The doors were closed, for everything was conducted with secrecy and solemnity. When the cover of the chalice had been removed and taken back to the recess in the rear of the Coenaculum, Jesus prayed and uttered some very solemn words. I saw that He was explaining the Last Supper to the Apostles, as also the ceremonies that were to accompany it. It reminded me of a priest teaching others the Holy Mass. During all this time, Jesus was becoming more and more recollected. He said to the Apostles that He was now about to give them all that He possessed, even His very Self. He seemed to be pouring out His whole Being in love, and I saw Him becoming perfectly transparent. He looked like a luminous apparition.

OUR FATHER

Our Father who art in heaven, hallowed be thy name. Thy kingdom come. Thy will be done, on earth as it is in heaven. Give us this day our daily bread; and forgive us our trespasses, as we forgive those who trespass against us; and lead us not into temptation, but deliver us from evil.

HAIL MARY XIO

Hail Mary full of Grace, the Lord is with thee. Blessed are thou among women and blessed is the fruit of thy womb Jesus. Holy Mary Mother of God, pray for us sinners now and at the hour of our death Amen.

MEDITATIONS

1) Before break of day Jesus, calling Peter and John, spoke to them at some length upon what they should order, what preparations they should make in Jerusalem for the eating of the Paschal lamb. The disciples had questioned Jesus the day before upon where this supper was to be held. Jesus told the two Apostles that they would, when ascending Mount Sion, meet a man carrying a water pitcher, one whom they already knew as he was the same that had attended to the Paschal meal for Jesus the year before at Bethania. They were to follow him into the house and say to him: "The Master asks us to tell you that His time is near at hand. He desires to celebrate the Pasch at your house". They should then ask to see the supper room, which they would find prepared, and there they should make ready all that was needed.

2) Judas spent the whole day in running around among the Pharisees and concerting his plans with them. The soldiers that were to apprehend Jesus were even shown him, and he so arranged his journey to and fro as to be able to account for his absence. Just before it was time for the Paschal Supper, he returned to the Lord. I have seen all his thoughts and plans. When Jesus spoke about him to Mary, I saw many things connected with his character and behaviour. He was active and obliging, but full of avarice, ambition, and envy, which passions he struggled not to control. He had even performed miracles and, in Jesus' absence, healed the sick. When Jesus

made known to the Blessed Virgin what was about to happen to Himself in His passion, she besought Him in touching terms to let her die with Him. But He exhorted her to bear her grief more calmly than the other women, telling her at the same time that He would rise again, and He named the spot upon which He would appear to her. This time she did not shed so many tears, though she was sad beyond expression and there was something awe-inspiring in her deep gravity. Like a devoted Son, Jesus thanked her for all her love. He embraced her with His right arm and pressed her to His breast. He told her that He would celebrate His Last Supper with her in spirit, and named the hour at which she should receive His Body and Blood.

3) Jesus and His followers ate the Paschal lamb in the Coenaculum in three separate groups of twelve, each presided over by one who acted as host. Jesus and the Twelve Apostles ate in the hall itself; In one of the side buildings near the entrance into the court of the Coenaculum, the holy women took their meal. Three lambs had been immolated and sprinkled for them in the Temple. But the fourth was slaughtered and sprinkled in the Coenaculum, and it was this that Jesus ate with The Twelve. Judas was not aware of this circumstance. He had been engaged in various business affairs, among which was the plot to betray the Lord, and consequently had arrived only a few moments before the repast, and after the immolation of the lamb had taken place.

4) The slaughter of the lamb for Jesus and the Apostles presented a scene most touching. It took place in the ante-room of the Coenaculum, Simeon's son, the Levite, assisting at it. The Apostles and disciples were present chanting the 118th Psalm. Jesus spoke of a new period then beginning, and said that the sacrifice of Moses and the signification of the Paschal lamb were about to be fulfilled, that on this account the lamb was to be immolated as formerly in Egypt, and that now in reality were they to go forth from the house of bondage. All the necessary vessels and instruments were now prepared. Then a beautiful little lamb was brought in, around its neck a garland which was taken off and sent to the Blessed Virgin, who was at some distance with the other women. The lamb was then bound, its back to a little board, with a cord passed around the body. It reminded me of Jesus bound to the pillar. Simeon's son held the lamb's head up, and Jesus stuck it in the neck with a knife, which He then handed to Simeon's son that he might complete the slaughter. Jesus appeared timid in wounding the lamb, as if it cost Him pain. His movement was quick, His manner grave. The blood was caught in a basin, and the attendants brought a branch of hyssop, which Jesus dipped into it. Then stepping to the door of the hall, He signed the two posts and the lock with the blood, and stuck the bloody branch above the lintel. He then uttered some solemn words, saying among other things: "The destroying angel shall pass by here. Without fear or anxiety you shall adore in this place when I, the true Paschal Lamb, shall have been immolated. A new era and a

new sacrifice is now about to begin, and they shall last till the end of the world".

5) Jesus in a few words reproved the Apostles for the strife that had arisen among them. He said among other things that He Himself was their servant, and that they should take their places on the seats for Him to wash their feet. They obeyed, observing the same order as at table. They sat on the backs of the seats, which were arranged in a half-circle, and rested their bare feet upon the seat itself. Jesus went from one to another and, from the basin held under them by John, with His hand scooped up water over the feet presented to Him. Then taking in both hands the long end of the towel with which He was girded, He passed it over the feet to dry them, and then moved on with James to the next. John emptied the water after each one into the large basin in the centre of the room, and then returned to the Lord with the empty one. Then Jesus again poured water from the bottle held by James over the feet of the next, and so on. During the whole of the Paschal Supper, the Lord's demeanour was most touching and gracious, and at this humble washing of His Apostles feet, He was full of love. He did not perform it as if it were a mere ceremony, but like a sacred act of love spring-ing straight from the heart. By it He wanted to give expres-sion to the love that burned within.

6) Jesus blessed the Passover loaves and, I think, the oil also that was standing near, elevated the plate of bread with both hands, raised His eyes toward Heaven, prayed, offered, set it

down on the table, and again covered it. Again Jesus prayed and taught. His words, glowing with fire and light, came forth from His mouth and entered into all the Apostles, excepting Judas. He took the plate with the morsels of bread and said, "Take and eat. This is My Body which is given for you". While saying these words, He stretched forth His right hand over it, as if giving a blessing, and as He did so, a brilliant light emanated from Him. His words were luminous as also the Bread, which as a body of light entered the mouth of the Apostles. It was as if Jesus Himself flowed into them. I saw all of them penetrated with light, bathed in light.

7) Judas alone was in darkness. Jesus presented the Bread first to Peter, then to John, and next made a sign to Judas, who was sitting diagonally from Him, to approach. Thus Judas was the third to whom Jesus presented the Blessed Sacrament, but it seemed as if the word of the Lord turned back from the mouth of the traitor. I was so terrified at the sight that I cannot describe my feelings. Jesus said to Judas: "What you are about to do, do quickly".

8) Jesus next raised the chalice by its two handles to a level with His face, and pronounced into it the words of consecration. While doing so, He was wholly transfigured and, as it were, transparent. He was as if passing over into what He was giving. He caused Peter and John to drink from the chalice while yet in His hands, and then He set it down. Judas also (though of this I am not quite certain) partook of the chalice, but he did not return to his place, for he immediately left the

Coenaculum. The others thought that Jesus had given him some commission to execute. He left without prayer or thanksgiving. And here we may see what an evil it is to fail to give thanks for our daily bread and for the Bread that endures to life eternal.

9) Jesus' movements during the institution of the Most Blessed Sacrament were measured and solemn, preceded and followed by explanations and instructions. I saw the Apostles after each noting down some things in the little parchment rolls that they carried about them. Jesus' turning to the right and left was full of gravity, as He always was when engaged in prayer. Every action indicated the institution of the Holy Mass. I saw the Apostles, when approaching one another and in other parts of it, bowing as priests are accustomed to do. Jesus now gave to the Apostles an instruction full of mystery. He told them how they were to preserve the Blessed Sacrament in memory of Him until the end of the world, taught them the necessary forms for making use of and communicating It, and in what manner they were by degrees to teach and publish the Mystery. He told them likewise when they were to receive what remained of the consecrated Species, when to give some to the Blessed Virgin, and how to consecrate It themselves after He had sent them the Comforter.

10) From the centre of the table, where He was standing, Jesus stepped a little to one side and imposed hands upon Peter and John, first on their shoulders and then on their head. During this action, they joined their hands and crossed

their thumbs. As they bowed low before Him (and I am not sure that they did not kneel) the Lord anointed the thumb and forefinger of each of their hands with Chrism, and made the Sign of the Cross with it on their head. He told them that this anointing would remain with them to the end of the world. All that Jesus did at the institution of the Blessed Eucharist and the ordination of the Apostles was done very secretly, and was later on taught as a Mystery. It has to this day remained essentially in the Church, though she has, under the inspiration of the Holy Ghost, developed it according to her needs.

GLORY BE TO THE FATHER

Glory be to the Father and to the Son and to the Holy Spirit. As it was in the beginning is now, and ever shall be, world without end. Amen.

THE FATIMA PRAYER

O my Jesus, forgive us our sins, save us from the fires of hell, and lead all souls to Heaven, especially those in most need of Your Mercy.

CONCLUDING PRAYERS

Upon concluding the recitation of the Holy Rosary, the following prayers are customary, but others too may be added according to one's devotion and preference.

HAIL, HOLY QUEEN

Hail Holy Queen, Mother of Mercy, Hail our life our sweetness and our hope. To thee do we cry, poor banished children of Eve, to thee do we send up our sighs, mourning and weeping in this vale of tears. Turn then most gracious Advocate thine eyes of mercy towards us and after this our exile, show unto us the blessed fruit of thy womb, Jesus. O clement, O loving, O sweet Virgin Mary. Pray for us O holy Mother of God, that we may be made worthy of the promises of Christ.

Let us pray

O God Whose only begotten son by His life death and resurrection has purchased for us the rewards of eternal life, grant we beseech Thee that meditating on these mysteries of the most Holy Rosary of the Blessed Virgin Mary we may both imitate what they contain and obtain what they promise, through the same Christ our Lord. Amen.

PRAYER TO SAINT MICHAEL THE ARCHANGEL

Holy Michael, the Archangel, defend us in the day of battle. Be our safeguard against the wickedness and snares of the devil. May God rebuke him, we humbly pray; and do thou, O Prince of the heavenly hosts, by the power of God thrust down into hell Satan and all the evil spirits who wander through the world seeking the ruin of souls. Amen.

MEMORARE

Remember, O most gracious Virgin Mary, that never was it known that anyone who fled to thy protection, implored thy help, or sought thine intercession was left unaided. Inspired by this confidence, I fly unto thee, O Virgin of virgins, my mother; to thee do I come, before thee I stand, sinful and sorrowful. O Mother of the Word Incarnate, despise not my petitions, but in thy mercy hear and answer me. Amen.

May the Divine Assistance remain always with us, and may the souls of the faithful departed, through the mercy of God rest in peace. Amen.

THE HOPEFUL MYSTERIES

❧

The Creation of all Things in view of Christ and His Holy Incarnation

FRUIT OF THIS MYSTERY: AWE OF GOD'S PLAN.

I HAVE HAD A GREAT VISION ON THE MYSTERY OF HOLY mass and I have seen that whatever good has existed since creation is owing to it. I saw the A and the O, and how all is contained in the O. I understood the signification of the circle in the spherical form of the earth and the heavenly bodies—the aureola of apparitions, and the Sacred Host. The connection between the mysteries of the Incarnation, the Redemption, and the Holy Sacrifice of the Mass was also shown me, and I saw how Mary encompassed what the heavens themselves could not contain.

OUR FATHER

Our Father who art in heaven, hallowed be thy name. Thy kingdom come. Thy will be done, on earth as it is in heaven. Give us this day our daily bread; and forgive us our trespasses, as we forgive those who trespass against us; and lead us not into temptation, but deliver us from evil.

HAIL MARY XIO

Hail Mary full of Grace, the Lord is with thee. Blessed are thou among women and blessed is the fruit of thy womb Jesus. Holy Mary Mother of God, pray for us sinners now and at the hour of our death Amen.

MEDITATIONS

1) I saw spreading out before me a boundless, resplendent space, above which floated a globe of light shining like a sun. I felt that It was the Unity of the Trinity. In my own mind, I

named It the ONE VOICE, and I watched It producing Its effects. Below the globe of light arose concentric circles of radiant choirs of spirits, wondrously bright and strong and beautiful. At first all of the spirits were lost in contemplation out of self, but soon some of them rested in self. At that instant, I saw this part of the glittering choirs hurled down, their beauty sunk in darkness, while the others, thronging quickly together, filled up their vacant places. And now the good angels occupied a smaller space. I did not see them leaving their places to pursue and combat the fallen choirs. The bad angels rested in self and fell away, while those that did not follow their example thronged into their vacant places. All this was instantaneous.

2) Immediately after the prayer of the faithful choirs and that movement in the Godhead, I saw below me, not far from and to the right of the world of shadows, another dark globe arise. I fixed my eyes steadily upon it. I beheld it as if in movement, growing larger and larger. Bright spots were breaking out upon it and encircling it like luminous bands. Here and there, they stretched out into brighter, broader plains, and at that moment I saw the form of the land setting boundaries to the water. In the bright places I saw a movement as of life, and on the land I beheld vegetation springing forth and myriads of living things arising. And now all other parts of the picture faded. The sky became blue, the sun burst forth, but I saw only one part of the earth lighted up and shining. That spot was charming, glorious, and I thought: There's Paradise!

3) It was as if the sun rose higher in the heavens, as if bright morning were awakening. It was the first morning. No created being had any knowledge of it, and it seemed as if all those created things had been there forever in their unsullied innocence. As the sun rose higher, I saw the plants and trees growing larger and larger. The waters became clearer and holier, colours grew purer and brighter—all was unspeakably charming. Creation was not then as it is now. Plants and flowers and trees had other forms. They are wild and mis-shapen now compared with what they were, for all things are now thoroughly degenerate. I saw there roses, white and red, and I thought them symbols of Christ's Passion and our Redemption. I saw also palm trees and others, high and spreading which cast their branches afar, as if forming roofs.

4) I saw Adam created, not in Paradise, but in the region in which Jerusalem was subsequently situated. I saw him come forth glittering and white from a mound of yellow earth, as if out of a mold. And now I saw Adam borne up on high to a garden, to Paradise. I saw Adam in Paradise among the plants and flowers, and not far from the fountain that played in its centre. He was awaking, as if from sleep. Although his person was more like to flesh than to spirit, yet he was dazzlingly white. He wondered at nothing, nor was he astonished at his own existence. Near the tree by the water arose a hill. On it I saw Adam reclining on his left side, his left hand under his cheek. God sent a deep sleep on him and he was rapt in vision. Then from his right side, from the same place in which the side of Jesus was opened by the lance, God drew

Eve. I saw her small and delicate. But she quickly increased in size until full-grown. She was exquisitely beautiful. Were it not for the Fall, all would be born in the same way, in tranquil slumber. Adam stretched forth his hand to Eve. They left the charming spot of Eve's creation and went through Paradise, looking at everything, rejoicing in everything. That place was the highest in Paradise. All was more radiant, more resplendent there than elsewhere.

5) When Eve had been formed, I saw that God gave something, or allowed something to flow upon Adam. It was as if there streamed from the Godhead, apparently in human form, currents of light from forehead, mouth, breast, and hands. They united in a globe of light which entered Adam's right side from where Eve had been taken. Adam alone received it. It was the germ of God's Blessing, which was threefold. The Blessing that Abraham received from the angel was one. It was of similar form, but not so luminous.

7) I saw Adam's heart very much the same as in men of the present day, but his breast was surrounded by rays of light. In the middle of his heart, I saw a sparkling halo of glory. In it was a tiny figure as if holding something in its hand. I think it symbolised the Third Person of the Godhead. From the hands and feet of Adam and Eve, shot rays of light. Their hair fell in five glittering tresses, two from the temples, two behind the ears, and one from the back of the head. I have always thought that by the Wounds of Jesus there were opened anew in the human body portals closed by Adam's

sin. I have been given to understand that Longinus opened in Jesus' Side the gate of regeneration to eternal life, therefore no one entered Heaven while that gate was closed.

8) The glittering beams on Adam's head denoted his abundant fruitfulness, his glory- a shining beauty which is restored to glorified souls and bodies. Our hair is the ruined, the extinct glory; and as is this hair of ours to rays of light, so is our present flesh to that of Adam before the Fall. The sunbeams around Adam's mouth bore reference to a holy posterity from God, which, had it not been for the Fall, would have been effectuated by the spoken word.

9) In the centre of the glittering garden, I saw a sheet of water in which lay an island connected with the opposite land by a pier. Both island and pier were covered with beautiful trees, but in the middle of the former stood one more magnificent than the others. It towered high over them as if guarding them. Its roots extended over the whole island as did also its branches, which were broad below and tapering to a point above. Its boughs were horizontal, and from them arose others like little trees. The leaves were fine, the fruit yellow, resting in a leafy calyx like a budding rose. It was something like a cedar. I do not remember ever having seen Adam, Eve, or any animal near that tree on the island. But I saw beautiful noble-looking white birds and heard them singing in its branches. That Tree was the Tree of Life.

10) The first man was an image of God, he was like Heaven; all was one in him, all was one with him. His form was a reproduction of the Divine Prototype. He was destined to possess and to enjoy earth and all created things, but holding them from God and giving thanks for them.

GLORY BE TO THE FATHER

Glory be to the Father and to the Son and to the Holy Spirit. As it was in the beginning is now, and ever shall be, world without end. Amen.

THE FATIMA PRAYER

O my Jesus, forgive us our sins, save us from the fires of hell, and lead all souls to Heaven, especially those in most need of Your Mercy.

The Promise of the Redeemer and Co-Redemptrix

THE FRUIT OF THIS MYSTERY:
GRATITUDE TO GOD.

ONCE WHEN THE DISASTER OF THE FALL WAS SHOWN ME in symbolical pictures, I saw Eve in the act of issuing from Adam's side, and even then stretching out her neck after the forbidden fruit. She ran quickly to the tree and clasped it in her arms. In an opposite picture, I saw Jesus born of the Immaculate Virgin. He ran straight to the Cross and embraced it. I saw posterity obscured and ruined by Eve, but again purified by the Passion of Jesus. By the pains of penance must the evil love of self be rooted out of the flesh.

OUR FATHER

Our Father who art in heaven, hallowed be thy name. Thy kingdom come. Thy will be done, on earth as it is in heaven. Give us this day our daily bread; and forgive us our trespasses, as we forgive those who trespass against us; and lead us not into temptation, but deliver us from evil.

HAIL MARY X10

Hail Mary full of Grace, the Lord is with thee. Blessed are thou among women and blessed is the fruit of thy womb Jesus. Holy Mary Mother of God, pray for us sinners now and at the hour of our death Amen.

MEDITATIONS

1) I saw the Fall of the angels in my childhood and ever after, day and night, I dreaded their influence. I thought they must do great harm to the earth, for they are always around it. It is well they have no bodies, else they would obscure the light of the sun. We should see them floating around us like shadows. After that action on the part of the angelic choirs, I felt assured that they would remain steadfast, that they would never fall away. It was made known to me that God in His judgement, in His eternal sentence against the rebel angels,

decreed the reign of strife until their vacant thrones are filled. But to fill those thrones seemed to me almost impossible, for it would take so long. The strife will, however, be upon the earth. There will be no strife above, for God has so ordained. After I had received this assurance, I could no longer sympathize with Lucifer, for I saw that he had cast himself down by his own free, wicked will. Neither could I feel such anger against Adam. On the contrary, I felt great sympathy for him because I thought: It has been thus ordained. I saw Eve draw near to Adam, and offer him the fruit. The interior of the fruit was blood-red and full of veins. I saw Adam and Eve losing their brilliancy and diminishing in stature. It was as if the sun went down.

2) By the reception of the fruit, Adam and Eve became, as it were, intoxicated, and their consent to sin wrought in them a great change. It was the serpent in them. Its nature pervaded theirs, and then came the tares among the wheat. Once man was endowed with the kingship of nature, but now all in him has become nature. He is now one of its slaves, a master conquered and fettered. He must now struggle and fight with nature—but I cannot clearly express it. It was as if man once possessed all things in God, their Creator and their Centre; but now he made himself their centre, and they became his master.

3) Once I had a great and connected vision of sin and the whole plan of Redemption. I saw all mysteries clearly and distinctly, but it is impossible for me to put all into words. I

saw sin in its innumerable ramifications from the Fall of the angels and from Adam's Fall down to the present day, and I saw all the preparations for the repairing and redeeming down to the coming and death of Jesus. Jesus showed me the extraordinary blending, the intrinsic uncleanness of all creatures, as well as all that He had done from the very beginning for their purification and restoration.

4) Mankind at first numbered two, then three, and at last they became innumerable. They had been images of God; but after the Fall, they became images of self, which images originated in sin. Sin placed them in communication with the fallen angels. They sought all their good in self and the creatures around them with all of whom the fallen angels had connection; and from that interminable blending, that sinking of his noble faculties in self and in fallen nature, sprang manifold wickedness and misery.

5) My spouse showed me this clearly, distinctly, intelligibly, more clearly than one beholds the things of daily life. At the time, I thought that a child might comprehend it, but now I cannot repeat it. He showed me the whole plan of Redemption with the way in which it was to be effected, as also all that He Himself had done. I saw that it is not right to say that God need not have become man, need not have died for us upon the Cross. I saw that He did what He did in conformity with His own infinite perfection, His mercy, and His justice; and yet that there is indeed no necessity in God, He does what He does, He is what He is!

6) After the Fall of Man, God made known to the angels His plan for the restoration of the human race. I saw the throne of God. I saw the Most Holy Trinity and a movement in the Divine Persons. I saw the nine choirs of angels and God announcing to them the way by which He would restore the fallen race. I saw the inexpressible joy and jubilation of the angels at the announcement. Above the angels in Heaven, I saw the image of the Virgin. It was not Mary in time; it was Mary in eternity, Mary in God.

7) I saw in pictures the mystery of Redemption from the Promise down to the fullness of time, and in side pictures I saw counteracting influences at work. At last, over the shining rock, I saw a large and magnificent church. It was the One, Holy, Catholic Church, which bears living in itself the salvation of the whole world. The connection of these pictures one with another and their transition from one to another was wonderful. Even what was evil and opposed to the end in view, even what was rejected by the angels as unfit, was made subservient to the development of Redemption.

8) I saw Melchisedech as an angel and a type of Jesus, as a priest upon the earth; inasmuch as the priesthood is in God, he was an angel priest of the eternal hierarchy. I saw him preparing, founding, building up, and separating the human family, and acting toward them as a guide. I saw too, Enoch and Noah, what they represented, what they effected; on the other side, I saw the ever-active empire of Hell and the infinitely varied manifestations and effects of an earthly,

carnal, diabolical idolatry. And I saw in all these manifestations similar pestiferous forms and figures leading, so to say, by a secret, inborn necessity and an uninterrupted process of dissolution to sin and corruption. In this manner, I saw sin and the prophetic, foreshadowing figures of Redemption which, in their way, were images of divine power as man himself in the image of God. All were shown me from Abraham to Moses, from Moses to the Prophets, also the way in which they were connected and their reference to similar types in our own day.

9) I saw Adam and Eve reach the earth, their place of penance. Oh, what a touching sight—those two creatures expiating their fault upon the naked earth! Adam had been allowed to bring an olive branch with him from Paradise, and now he planted it. Later on, the Cross was made from its wood. Adam and Eve were unspeakably sad. Where I saw them, they could scarcely get a glimpse of Paradise, and they were constantly descending lower and lower. It seemed as if something revolved and they came at last, through night and darkness, to the wretched, miserable place upon which they had to do penance.

10) At last, I saw a vision on earth such as God had shown to Adam; that is, that a Virgin would arise and restore to him the salvation he had forfeited. Adam knew not when it would take place, and I saw his deep sadness because Eve bore him only sons. But at last she had a daughter.

GLORY BE TO THE FATHER

Glory be to the Father and to the Son and to the Holy Spirit. As it was in the beginning is now, and ever shall be, world without end. Amen.

THE FATIMA PRAYER

O my Jesus, forgive us our sins, save us from the fires of hell, and lead all souls to Heaven, especially those in most need of Your Mercy.

The Birth of the Immaculate Virgin Mary to Sts. Joachim and Anne

THE FRUIT OF THIS MYSTERY:
LOVE OF HOLY PURITY.

WHEN MARY WAS BORN, I SAW HER AT ONE AND THE same time before the Most Holy Trinity in Heaven and on earth in Anne's arms. I saw the joy of the whole heavenly court. I saw all her gifts and graces in a supernatural way revealed to her. I often have such visions, but they are for me inexpressible, for others unintelligible, therefore am I silent with regard to them. Mary was also instructed in innumerable mysteries. As this vision ended, the child cried upon earth. I saw the news of Mary's birth announced also in Limbo, and I beheld the transports of joy with which it was received by the Patriarchs, especially by Adam and Eve who rejoiced that the Promise made them in Paradise was now fulfilled. I saw also that the Patriarchs increased in grace, their abode became lighter and less constrained, and that they began to exercise a greater influence on earth. It was as if all their good works, all their penance, all the efforts of their life, all their desires and aspirations had at last brought forth fruit. All nature, animate and inanimate, men and beasts were stirred to joy, and I heard sweet singing. But sinners were filled with anguish and remorse. I saw, especially around Nazareth and in other parts of Palestine, many possessed souls who at the hour of Mary's birth became perfectly furious. They uttered horrible cries, and they were tossed and dashed about. The devils cried out of them: "We must go forth! A virgin is born, and there are upon earth so many angels who torment us. We must go forth, and never again shall we dare possess these human beings!".

OUR FATHER

Our Father who art in heaven, hallowed be thy name. Thy kingdom come. Thy will be done, on earth as it is in heaven. Give us this day our daily bread; and forgive us our trespasses, as we forgive those who trespass against us; and lead us not into temptation, but deliver us from evil.

HAIL MARY XIO

Hail Mary full of Grace, the Lord is with thee. Blessed are thou among women and blessed is the fruit of thy womb Jesus. Holy Mary Mother of God, pray for us sinners now and at the hour of our death Amen.

MEDITATIONS

1) Among the angels, I noticed a kind of monstrance at which all were working. It was in shape like a tower, and on it were all kinds of mysterious carvings. Near it on either side stood two figures, their joined hands embracing it. At every instant it became larger and more magnificent. I saw something from God passing through the angelic choirs and going into the monstrance. It was a shining Holy Thing, and it became more clearly defined the nearer it drew to the monstrance. It appeared to me to be the germ of the divine Blessing for a pure offspring which had been given to Adam, but withdrawn when he was on the point of responding to Eve and consenting to eat the forbidden fruit. It was the Blessing that was again bestowed upon Abraham, withdrawn from Jacob, by Moses deposited in the Ark of the Covenant, and lastly received by Joachim, the father of Mary, in order that Mary might be as pure and stainless in her Conception as was Eve upon coming forth from the side of the sleeping Adam.

2) Anne was especially dear to her parents. I saw her as a child. She was not strikingly beautiful, though prettier than some others. Her beauty was not to be compared with Mary's, but she was extraordinarily pious, childlike, and innocent. She was the same at every age, as I have seen, as a maiden, as a mother, and as a little old grandmother. Whenever I happened to see a very childlike old peasant woman, I always thought: "She is like Anne". When in her fifth year, Anne was taken to the Temple as Mary was later. There she remained twelve years, returning home in her seventeenth year. About eighteen months after, Anne, then in her nineteenth year, married Heli, or Joachim, This she did in obedience to the spiritual direction of a Prophet. On account of the approach of the Saviour's advent, she married Joachim of the House of David, for Mary was to belong to the House of David; otherwise she would have had to choose her spouse from among the Levites of the tribe of Aaron, as all of her race had done. She had had many suitors and, at the time of the Prophet's decision, she was not yet acquainted with Joachim. She chose him only upon supernatural direction.

3) And now the holy couple began married life. Their only aim was by a life pleasing to God, to attract upon themselves that blessing for which alone they sighed. I saw them both going to and fro among their herds. They divided them into three parts, and drove the best to the Temple. The poor received the second part, and the worst was retained for themselves. They acted in the same manner with all that belonged to them.

4) Anne had the assurance, the firm belief that the coming of the Messiah was very near, and that she herself would be of the number of His relatives according to the flesh. Her prayer was continuous and she constantly aimed at greater purity. It had been revealed to her that she was to bring forth a child of benediction. For nineteen years and five months after the birth of this first child, Joachim and Anne were childless. They lived in continued prayer and sacrifice, in mortification and continence.

5) The anxiety of both and their longing after the promised blessing had reached its height. Many of their acquaintances upbraided them because of their sterility, which they attributed to some wickedness. Joachim often remained far away with his flock, when Anne had long besought God not to separate her from Joachim, her pious husband, although He had been pleased to deprive her of children, an angel appeared to her. He hovered above her in the air. He told her to set her heart at rest, for the Lord had heard her prayer; that she should on the following morning go with two of her maid servants to the Temple of Jerusalem; that there under the Golden Gate, entering by the side of the valley of Josaphat, she should meet Joachim, who was even now on his way there, that Joachim's offering would be accepted, that his prayer would be heard, and that he, (the angel), had appeared also to him. The angel likewise directed Anne to take some doves with her as an offering, and promised that the name of the child she was soon to conceive should be made known to her.

6) Anne thanked the Lord and returned to the house. When, after her lengthy prayer, she lay on her couch asleep I saw light descending upon her. It surrounded her, yes, even penetrated her. I saw her, upon an interior perception, tremblingly awake and sit upright. Near her, to the right, she saw a luminous figure writing on the wall in large, shining Hebrew characters. I read and understood the writing word for word. It was to this effect: that she should conceive, that the fruit of her womb should be altogether special, and that the Blessing received by Abraham was to be the source of this conception. I saw Anne's anxiety as to how she should communicate all that to Joachim; but the angel reassured her by telling her of Joachim's vision.

7) The angel spoke to Joachim, "Anne will conceive an immaculate child from whom the Redeemer of the world will be born". The angel told him moreover not to grieve over his sterility which was not a disgrace to him, but a glory, for that what his spouse would conceive should not be from him but through him, a fruit from God, the culminating point of the Blessing given to Abraham. I saw that Joachim could not comprehend these words. Then the angel led him behind the curtain that concealed the grating before the Holy of Holies. The space between the curtain and the grating afforded standing room. Then the angel held up before Joachim's face a shining ball that reflected like a mirror. Joachim breathed upon it and gazed into it. I saw it hovering in the air and, as if through an opening, innumerable and wonderful pictures went into it. They were like a whole world, one picture

growing out of another. Up in the highest point appeared the Most Holy Trinity, and below, to one side, were Paradise, Adam and Eve, the Fall, the Promise of a Redeemer, Noah, the Ark, scenes connected with Abraham and Moses, the Ark of the Covenant, and numerous symbols of Mary. I saw cities, towers, gateways, flowers, all wonderfully connected together by beams of light like bridges. They were all assaulted and combated by beasts and spirits, which, however, were everywhere beaten back by the streams of light that burst upon them.

8) I saw Joachim and Anne embrace each other in ecstasy. They were surrounded by hosts of angels, some floating over them carrying a luminous tower like that which we see in the pictures of the Litany of Loretto. The tower vanished between Joachim and Anne, both of whom were encompassed by brilliant light and glory. At the same moment the heavens above them opened, and I saw the joy of the Most Holy Trinity and of the angels over the Conception of Mary. Both Joachim and Anne were in a supernatural state. I learned that, at the moment in which they embraced and the light shone around them, the Immaculate Conception of Mary was accomplished. I was also told that Mary was conceived just as conception would have been effected, were it not for the fall of man.

9) Anne felt that her time was near, and she desired for the female relatives to pray with her. They all withdrew behind a curtain that concealed an oratory. Anne opened the doors of

a little closet built in the wall. Anne knelt before the shrine, one of the women on either side, and the third behind her. Again I heard them reciting a Psalm. I think that the burning bush on Horeb was mentioned in it. And now a supernatural light began to fill the chamber and to hover around Anne. The three women fell prostrate as if stunned. Around Anne the light took the exact form of the thorn bush on Horeb, so that I could no longer see her. The flame streamed inward, and all at once I saw Anne receiving into her arms the shining child Mary. She wrapped it in her mantle, pressed it to her heart, laid it on the stool before the relics, and went on with her prayer.

10) Then I heard the child crying, and I saw Anne drawing forth some linen from under the large veil that enveloped her. She swathed the child first in grey and then in red, leaving the breast, arms, and head bare, and then the luminous thorn bush vanished. The holy women arose and in glad surprise received the newborn child into their arms. They wept for joy. All intoned a hymn of praise while Anne held the child on high. I saw the chamber again filled with light and myriads of angels. They announced the child's name, singing: "On the twentieth day, this child shall be called Mary". Then they sang Gloria and Alleluia. I heard all these words. One of the women went and called Joachim. He entered, knelt by Anne's couch, and his tears fell in torrents over the child. Then he took it up, held it aloft, and intoned a canticle of praise like unto that of Zechariah. He spoke words expressive of his longing now to die, and he alluded to the Blessing

given by God to Abraham and perfected in himself, also to the root of Jesse.

GLORY BE TO THE FATHER

Glory be to the Father and to the Son and to the Holy Spirit. As it was in the beginning is now, and ever shall be, world without end. Amen.

THE FATIMA PRAYER

O my Jesus, forgive us our sins, save us from the fires of hell, and lead all souls to Heaven, especially those in most need of Your Mercy.

The Presentation of Mary in the Temple as a Girl

THE FRUIT OF THIS MYSTERY:
THE GIFT OF PIETY.

AS MARY ENTERED THE TEMPLE, I SAW ABOVE THE HEART of Mary the glory and the Mystery of the Ark of the Covenant. At first it looked exactly like the Ark of the Covenant; and lastly like the Temple itself. Out of the Mystery and before Mary's breast, arose a chalice similar to that of the Last Supper; above it and just in front of her mouth appeared bread marked with a cross. Beams of light radiated around her, and in them shone her various types and symbols. The mysterious pictures of the Litany of Loretto and the other names and titles of Mary, I saw ranged up the whole flight of steps and around her. From her shoulders, right and left, stretched an olive and a cedar branch crosswise above an elegant palm tree with a small tuft of leaves that stood directly behind her. In the intervening spaces of this verdant cross, appeared all the instruments of Christ's Passion. Over the vision hovered the Holy Spirit, a figure winged with glory, in appearance more human than dovelike. The heavens opened above Mary and the central point of the Heavenly Jerusalem, the City of God, floated over her with all the gardens, the palaces, and the dwellings of the future saints. Angels in myriads hovered around, and the glory that encircled her was full of angelic faces. Ah, who can express it! Infinite variety, unceasing change, all these pictures following quickly upon and, as it were, growing out of one another. Innumerable points of this vision, I have forgotten. All the splendour and magnificence of the Temple, the richly ornamented wall before which Mary was standing—all grew dark and sombre. The whole Temple disappeared, for Mary and her glory alone was visible.

OUR FATHER

Our Father who art in heaven, hallowed be thy name. Thy kingdom come. Thy will be done, on earth as it is in heaven. Give us this day our daily bread; and forgive us our trespass-

es, as we forgive those who trespass against us; and lead us not into temptation, but deliver us from evil.

HAIL MARY XIO

Hail Mary full of Grace, the Lord is with thee. Blessed are thou among women and blessed is the fruit of thy womb Jesus. Holy Mary Mother of God, pray for us sinners now and at the hour of our death Amen.

MEDITATIONS

1) Mary was three years and three months old when she made the vow to join the virgins in the Temple. She was very delicately built and had golden hair inclined to curl at the ends. She was already as tall as a child of five or six here in our country. I saw in Anne's house the preparations for Mary's admittance into the Temple. It was made the occasion of a great feast. Five priests had assembled from Nazareth, Sephoris, and other places, among them Zechariah and a son of the brother of Anne's father. They were about to perform a sacred ceremony over the child Mary, a kind of examination as to whether she was sufficiently mature in mind to be admitted to the Temple. Besides the priests, there were present Anne's sister from Sephoris and her older daughter, Mary Heli with her child, and several other little girls and relatives.

2) The robes worn by the child at this feast were cut out by the priests themselves and the different parts quickly sewed together by the women present. The child was clothed in them at certain periods when subjected to a series of interrogatories. The ceremony was in itself very grave and solemn, although the faces of the aged priests were at times lit up by smiles of admiration at the expressions and answers of the little Mary, and it was frequently interrupted by the tears of Joachim and Anne. Three entire suits were prepared for Mary and put on her at different times during the ceremony, the questioning and answering going on in the meantime. All this took place in a large room next to the dining hall.

3) The priests now put to the child all sorts of questions relative to the discipline enforced in the Temple. Mary now repeated her resolve to abstain from flesh, fish, and milk, to make use of only a certain drink prepared from the pith of a reed soaked in water. Mary expressed her resolution to refrain also from spices and fruits, with the exception of a kind of yellow berry that grows in bunches. I know them well. Children and poor people eat them in that country. She said also that she would lie on the bare ground and nightly rise three times to pray. Upon hearing this, Anne and Joachim shed tears, and the aged Joachim pressed his child in his arms, saying: "Ah, my child, that is too hard! If you live so mortified a life, I, your poor old father, shall never see you again". This scene was very affecting. The priests replied to the child that she should, like the others, rise once only

during the night, and they laid down other and milder conditions for her.

4) At last, Mary was blessed by the priests. I saw her radiant with light as she stood on the little altar throne, two priests on either side of her and one opposite. They held rolls of writing, and prayed over the child, their hands outstretched above her. At that moment, I saw a wonderful vision in the child Mary. She seemed, by virtue of the blessing, to become transparent. In her was a glory, a halo of unspeakable splendour, and in that halo appeared the Mystery of the Ark of the Covenant, as if in a glittering crystal vessel. I saw Mary's heart open like the doors of a temple, and the Holy Thing of the Ark of the Covenant, around which a tabernacle of precious stones of multiplied signification had been formed like a heavenly throne, going into her heart through that opening, like the Ark of the Covenant into the Holy of Holies, like the monstrance into the tabernacle. I saw that by this the child Mary was glorified; she hovered above the earth. With the entrance of this Sacrament into Mary's heart, which immediately closed over It, the vision faded, and I saw the child all penetrated by glowing fervour. During this wonderful vision, I saw that Zechariah received an interior assurance, a heavenly monition that Mary was the chosen vessel of the Mystery. From it he had received a ray that had appeared figuratively in Mary.

5) I saw Joachim, Anne, and their elder daughter busied during the night packing and preparing for the journey to

the temple. I saw also two boys present. They were not human. They appeared there supernaturally and with a spiritual signification. They carried long standards rolled upon staffs furnished with knobs at both ends. The larger of the two boys came to me with his standard unfurled, read, and explained it to me. The writing appeared entirely strange to me, the single, golden letters all inverted. One letter represented a whole word. The language sounded unfamiliar, but I understood it all the same. He showed me in his roll the passage referring to the burning thorn bush of Moses. He explained to me how the thorn bush burned, and yet was not consumed; so now was the child Mary inflamed with the fire of the Holy Spirit, but in her humility she knew nothing of it. It signifies also the Divinity and Humanity in Jesus, and how God's fire united with the child Mary. The putting-off of the shoes, he explained thus: "The Law will now be fulfilled. The veil is withdrawn and the essence appears". By the little standard on his staff was signified, as he told me, that Mary now began her course, her career, to become the Mother of the Redeemer. The other boy seemed to be playing with his standard. He jumped about and ran around with it. By this was signified Mary's innocence. The great Promise is to be fulfilled in her, rests upon her, and yet she plays like a child in this holy destiny. I cannot express the loveliness of those boys. They were different from all others present, and these latter did not appear to see them.

6) There were besides Anne about six female relatives with their children and some men who accompanied them. Joa-

chim guided the beast, upon which the child Mary sometimes rode. The little procession was accompanied by apparitions of the Prophets. As Mary hastened from the house, they
pointed out to me a place in their scrolls, wherein it was
declared that, although the Temple was indeed magnificent,
yet Mary contained in herself still greater magnificence. Mary
rejoiced at being now so near to the Temple. Joachim embraced her, weeping and saying, "I shall never see you again!"
During the repast, Mary went here and there. Several times
she reclined by Anne's side at table, or stood behind her with
her arm around her neck.

7) I saw the arrival of the procession in Jerusalem, Zechariah
and the other men had already gone to the Temple, and now
Mary was led there by the women and the virgins. Anne and
her elder daughter Mary Heli, with the little daughter of the
latter, Mary Cleophas, walked first; then came Mary in her
second suit, the sky-blue dress and mantle, her neck and arms
adorned with garlands, and the flower-wreathed candlestick
in her hand. On either side walked three little maidens with
similarly trimmed candlesticks. They were dressed in white
embroidered with gold, and wore bluish mantles. They were
quite covered with garlands, even their arms were twined
with flowers. Then followed the other virgins and little girls,
about twenty in number, all dressed beautifully, but somewhat differently, though all wore mantles.

8) After the sacrifice was offered, which Joachim had sup-
plied for, a portable altar was set up under the arched gate-

way, and before it were placed a couple of steps. Zechariah and Joachim, with some priests and two Levites, entered from the court of the altar of burnt offerings, carrying scrolls and writing materials, while Anne led Mary to the steps before the altar. Mary knelt upon the steps, while Joachim and Anne, laying their hands on her head, uttered some words bearing reference to the offering of their child, which words were written down by the two Levites. Then one of the priests cut a lock of hair from the child's head, and cast it upon a pan of live coals, after which he threw around her a brown veil. During this ceremony, the girls sang Psalm 44, Eructavit cor meum; the priests, Psalm 49, Deus deorum Dominus; and the boys played on their musical instruments.

9) And now the priests led the Holy Virgin up a long flight of steps in the wall that separated the sanctuary from the rest of the Temple. Behind Mary and on the other side of the wall, a priest was standing at the altar of incense, only half of his person visible from the point at which Mary and her attendants were placed. Through an opening contrived for the purpose, one could cast incense upon the altar without entering the court. The priest now at the incense altar was a holy old man. While he offered sacrifice and the cloud of incense arose around Mary, I saw a vision, which grew in magnitude until at last it filled the whole Temple and obscured it.

10) After the celebration amongst the girls of the temple, Mary was led to her cell, the one nearest to the Holy of

Holies. I had often seen the child Mary seized with holy longing for the Messiah and saying, "Oh, will the promised Child be born soon? Oh, if I could only see that Child! Oh, if only I am living when He is born!", and she would shed tears of longing for the promised Saviour. Mary was reared in the Temple under the care of the matrons and occupied herself with embroidery, with all kinds of ornamental work, and with cleansing the priestly garments and the vessels belonging to the Temple. From their cells the virgins could see into the Temple and would pray and meditate. They were, by the fact of their parents having placed them there, entirely dedicated to the Lord. Upon reaching a certain age, they were given in marriage, for there was among the more enlightened Israelites the pious, though secret hope that from such a virgin dedicated to God, the Messiah would be born.

GLORY BE TO THE FATHER

Glory be to the Father and to the Son and to the Holy Spirit. As it was in the beginning is now, and ever shall be, world without end. Amen.

THE FATIMA PRAYER

O my Jesus, forgive us our sins, save us from the fires of hell, and lead all souls to Heaven, especially those in most need of Your Mercy.

The Chaste Espousals
of Mary and Joseph

THE FRUIT OF THIS MYSTERY:
HONOUR OF THE HOLY CHASTITY OF ST. JOSEPH.

THE ESPOUSALS OF OUR LADY AND ST. JOSEPH TOOK place, I think, upon our 23rd of January. They were celebrated in Jerusalem, on Mount Zion in a house often used for such feasts. The seven virgins that were to leave the Temple with Mary, had already departed. They were recalled to accompany Mary on her festal journey to Nazareth, where Anne had already prepared her little home. The marriage feast lasted seven or eight days. The women and the virgins, companions of Mary in the Temple, were present, also many relatives of Joachim and Anne, and two daughters from Gophna. Many lambs were slaughtered and offered in sacrifice.

OUR FATHER

Our Father who art in heaven, hallowed be thy name. Thy kingdom come. Thy will be done, on earth as it is in heaven. Give us this day our daily bread; and forgive us our trespasses, as we forgive those who trespass against us; and lead us not into temptation, but deliver us from evil.

HAIL MARY XIO

Hail Mary full of Grace, the Lord is with thee. Blessed are thou among women and blessed is the fruit of thy womb Jesus. Holy Mary Mother of God, pray for us sinners now and at the hour of our death Amen.

MEDITATIONS

1) Joseph was the third of six brothers, his parents dwelt in a large mansion outside of Bethlehem. It was the ancient birthplace of David, but in Joseph's time only the principal

walls were in existence. His father's name was Jacob. By the time Joseph was perhaps eight years old he was very different from his brothers, very talented, and he learned quickly; but he was simple in his tastes, gentle, pious, and unambitious. The other boys used to play him all kinds of tricks and knock him around at will, but he bore it all patiently.

2) Joseph's parents were not well-satisfied with him. They would have wished him, on account of his talents, to fit himself for a position in the world. But he was too unworldly for such aims, he had no desire whatever to shine. He may have been about twelve years old when I often saw him beyond Bethlehem opposite the Crib Cave, praying with some very pious, old, Jewish women. Joseph was deeply pious; he prayed much for the coming of the Messiah.

3) Shortly before his call to Jerusalem for his espousals with Mary, Joseph entertained the idea of fitting up a more secluded oratory in his dwelling. But an angel appeared to him in prayer, and told him not to do it; that, as in ancient times, the Patriarch Joseph became by God's appointment the administrator of the Egyptian granaries, so now to him was the granary of Redemption to be wedded. In his humility Joseph could not comprehend the meaning of this and so he betook himself to prayer.

4) There were seven other virgins who were with Mary to be dismissed from the Temple and given in marriage. On this account St. Anne went to Jerusalem to be with Mary, who

grieved at the thought of leaving the Temple. But she was told that she must be married.

5) The priest prayed sitting before a scroll of writings, and in vision his hand was placed upon that verse in the Prophet Isaiah (Is. 11: 1) in which it is written that there shall come forth a rod out of the root of Jesse and a flower shall rise up out of his root.

6) There upon I saw that all the unmarried men in the country of the House of David were summoned to the Temple. Many of them made their appearance in holiday attire, and Mary was conducted to their presence. I saw one among them, a very pious youth from the region of Bethlehem, who had always ardently prayed to be allowed to minister to the advent of the Messiah. Great was his desire to wed Mary. But Mary wept; she wished not to take a husband. Then the high priest gave to each of the suitors a branch which was to be held in the hand during the offering of prayer and sacrifice. After that, all the branches were laid in the Holy of Holies with the understanding that he whose branch should blossom, was to be Mary's husband.

7) Now when that pious youth who so ardently desired to wed Mary found that this branch, along with all the others, had failed to blossom, he retired to a hall outside the Temple and, with arms raised to God, wept bitterly. The other suitors left the Temple, and that youth hurried to Mount Carmel where, since the days of Elias, hermits had dwelt. He took up

his abode on the mount, and there spent his days in prayer for the coming of the Messiah.

8) I saw the priests, after this, hunting through different rolls of writing in their search for another descendant of the House of David, one that had not presented himself among the suitors for Mary's hand. And there they found that, among the six brothers of Bethlehem, one was unknown and ignored. They sought him out and so discovered Joseph's retreat, six miles from Jerusalem, near Samaria. It was a small place on a little river. There Joseph dwelt alone in a humble house near the water, and carried on the trade of a carpenter under another master. He was told to go up to the Temple. He went, accordingly, arrayed in his best clothing. A branch was given him. As he was about to lay it upon the altar, it blossomed on top into a white flower like a lily. At the same time I saw a light like the Holy Spirit hovering over him. He was then led to Mary, who was in her chamber, and she accepted him as her spouse.

9) I have had a clear vision of Mary in her bridal dress. Anne had brought all the beautiful clothes, but Mary was so modest that it was only with reluctance that she allowed herself to be arrayed in them. The Blessed Virgin had auburn hair, dark eyebrows, fine and arched, a very high forehead, large downcast eyes with long, dark lashes, a straight nose, and a lovely mouth around which played a most noble expression. She was of medium height, and she moved very gently and gravely, looking very bashful in her rich attire.

10) Afterwards I saw Joseph and Mary in the house of Nazareth. Joseph had a separate apartment in the front of the house, a three-cornered chamber this side of the kitchen. Both Mary and Joseph were timid and reserved in each other's presence. They were very quiet and prayerful.

GLORY BE TO THE FATHER

Glory be to the Father and to the Son and to the Holy Spirit. As it was in the beginning is now, and ever shall be, world without end. Amen.

THE FATIMA PRAYER

O my Jesus, forgive us our sins, save us from the fires of hell, and lead all souls to Heaven, especially those in most need of Your Mercy.

CONCLUDING PRAYERS

Upon concluding the recitation of the Holy Rosary, the following prayers are customary, but others too may be added according to one's devotion and preference.

HAIL, HOLY QUEEN

Hail Holy Queen, Mother of Mercy, Hail our life our sweetness and our hope. To thee do we cry, poor banished children of Eve, to thee do we send up our sighs, mourning and weeping in this vale of tears. Turn then most gracious Advocate thine eyes of mercy towards us and after this our exile, show unto us the blessed fruit of thy womb, Jesus. O clement, O loving, O sweet Virgin Mary. Pray for us O holy Mother of God, that we may be made worthy of the promises of Christ.

Let us pray

O God Whose only begotten son by His life death and resurrection has purchased for us the rewards of eternal life, grant we beseech Thee that meditating on these mysteries of the most Holy Rosary of the Blessed Virgin Mary we may both imitate what they contain and obtain what they promise, through the same Christ our Lord. Amen.

PRAYER TO SAINT MICHAEL THE ARCHANGEL

Holy Michael, the Archangel, defend us in the day of battle. Be our safeguard against the wickedness and snares of the devil. May God rebuke him, we humbly pray; and do thou, O Prince of the heavenly hosts, by the power of God thrust down into hell Satan and all the evil spirits who wander through the world seeking the ruin of souls. Amen.

MEMORARE

Remember, O most gracious Virgin Mary, that never was it known that anyone who fled to thy protection, implored thy help, or sought thine intercession was left unaided. Inspired by this confidence, I fly unto thee, O Virgin of virgins, my mother; to thee do I come, before thee I stand, sinful and sorrowful. O Mother of the Word Incarnate, despise not my petitions, but in thy mercy hear and answer me. Amen.

May the Divine Assistance remain always with us, and may the souls of the faithful departed, through the mercy of God rest in peace. Amen.

PRAYERS

SIGN OF THE CROSS

In the name of the Father, and of the Son, and of the Holy Spirit. Amen.

THE APOSTLES' CREED

I believe in God the Father Almighty, Creator of heaven and earth; and in Jesus Christ, His only Son, our Lord; Who was conceived by the Holy Ghost, born of the Virgin Mary, suffered under Pontius Pilate, was crucified, died and was buried. He descended into hell. On the third day He arose again; He ascended into heaven, and sitteth at the right hand of God, the Father Almighty; from thence He shall come to judge the living and the dead. I believe in the Holy Ghost, the Holy Catholic Church, the communion of saints, the forgivness of sins, the resurrection of the body, and life everlasting. Amen.

OUR FATHER

Our Father who art in heaven, hallowed be thy name. Thy kingdom come. Thy will be done, on earth as it is in heaven. Give us this day our daily bread; and forgive us our trespasses, as we forgive those who trespass against us; and lead us not into temptation, but deliver us from evil.

HAIL MARY

Hail Mary full of Grace, the Lord is with thee. Blessed are thou among women and blessed is the fruit of thy womb Jesus. Holy Mary Mother of God, pray for us sinners now and at the hour of our death Amen.

GLORY BE TO THE FATHER

Glory be to the Father and to the Son and to the Holy Spirit. As it was in the beginning is now, and ever shall be, world without end. Amen.

THE FATIMA PRAYER

O my Jesus, forgive us our sins, save us from the fires of hell, and lead all souls to Heaven, especially those in most need of Your Mercy.

CONCLUDING PRAYERS

Upon concluding the recitation of the Holy Rosary, the following prayers are customary, but others too may be added according to one's devotion and preference.

HAIL, HOLY QUEEN

Hail Holy Queen, Mother of Mercy, Hail our life our sweetness and our hope. To thee do we cry, poor banished children of Eve, to thee do we send up our sighs, mourning and weeping in this vale of tears. Turn then most gracious Advocate thine eyes of mercy towards us and after this our exile, show unto us the blessed fruit of thy womb, Jesus. O clement, O loving, O sweet Virgin Mary. Pray for us O holy Mother of God, that we may be made worthy of the promises of Christ.

Let us pray

O God Whose only begotten son by His life death and resurrection has purchased for us the rewards of eternal life, grant we beseech Thee that meditating on these mysteries of the most Holy Rosary of the Blessed Virgin Mary we may both imitate what they contain and obtain what they promise, through the same Christ our Lord. Amen.

PRAYER TO SAINT MICHAEL THE ARCHANGEL

Holy Michael, the Archangel, defend us in the day of battle. Be our safeguard against the wickedness and snares of the devil. May God rebuke him, we humbly pray; and do thou, O Prince of the heavenly hosts, by the power of God thrust down into hell Satan and all the evil spirits who wander through the world seeking the ruin of souls. Amen.

MEMORARE

Remember, O most gracious Virgin Mary, that never was it known that anyone who fled to thy protection, implored thy help, or sought thine intercession was left unaided. Inspired by this confidence, I fly unto thee, O Virgin of virgins, my mother; to thee do I come, before thee I stand, sinful and sorrowful. O Mother of the Word Incarnate, despise not my petitions, but in thy mercy hear and answer me. Amen.

May the Divine Assistance remain always with us, and may the souls of the faithful departed, through the mercy of God rest in peace. Amen.

CATHOLIC WAY PUBLISHING

QUALITY PAPERBACKS AND E-BOOKS

TRUE DEVOTION TO MARY: WITH PREPARATION FOR TOTAL CONSECRATION
BY SAINT LOUIS DE MONTFORT

> 6" x 9" Hardback: ISBN–13: 978–1–78379–004–3
> 6" x 9" Paperback: ISBN–13: 978–1–78379–011–1
> 5" x 8" Paperback: ISBN–13: 978–1–78379–000–5
> MOBI E-Book: ISBN–13: 978–1–78379–001–2
> EPUB E-Book: ISBN–13: 978–1–78379–002–9

THE SECRET OF THE ROSARY BY SAINT LOUIS DE MONTFORT

> 5" x 8" Paperback: ISBN–13: 978–1–78379–310–5
> MOBI E-Book: ISBN–13: 978–1–78379–311–2
> EPUB E-Book: ISBN–13: 978–1–78379–312–9

THE IMITATION OF CHRIST BY THOMAS A KEMPIS

> 5" x 8" Paperback: ISBN–13: 978–1–78379–037–1
> MOBI E-Book: ISBN–13: 978–1–78379–038–8
> EPUB E-Book: ISBN–13: 978–1–78379–039–5

MY DAILY PRAYERS BY CATHOLIC WAY PUBLISHING

> 5" x 8" Paperback: ISBN–13: 978–1–78379–027–2
> MOBI E-Book: ISBN–13: 978–1–78379–028–9
> EPUB E-Book: ISBN–13: 978–1–78379–029–6

THE MYSTICAL CITY OF GOD: POPULAR ABRIDGEMENT
BY VENERABLE MARY OF AGREDA

> 5" x 8" Paperback: ISBN–13: 978–1–78379–063–0
> MOBI E-Book: ISBN–13: 978–1–78379–064–7
> EPUB E-Book: ISBN–13: 978–1–78379–065–4

CATHOLIC WAY
PUBLISHING

www.catholicwaypublishing.com
London, England, UK
2019

42098289R00137

Printed in Poland
by Amazon Fulfillment
Poland Sp. z o.o., Wrocław